Also by Rebecca J. Bastian
~*~
Crater Lake Lodge: Through the Kitchen Door

The Spirit of America

~ Back to Basics ~

The Spirit of America

~ Back to Basics ~

REBECCA J. BASTIAN

The Spirit of America: Back to Basics
Copyright 2021
Rebecca J. Bastian

All rights reserved. No part of this publication may be reproduced, stored in a retrieval system, or transmitted in any form or by any means electronic, mechanical, photocopying, recording, or otherwise without the prior written permission of the publisher and copyright owner.

All Scripture quotations are taken from The Holy Bible, English Standard Version. Copyright 2001 by Crossway, a publishing ministry of Good News Publishers.

Printed in the United States of America.

ISBN: 978-0-578-92343-7

Dedicated to:

Non-Com. Adam Henning, PA
Sgt. Christophel Henning Sr., PA
Sgt. John Reeves, NJ
and to any of my other ancestors who fought in the American Revolution.

"The time is now near at hand which must probably determine, whether Americans are to be, Freemen, or Slaves; whether they are to have any property they can call their own; whether their Houses, and Farms, are to be pillaged and destroyed, and they consigned to a State of Wretchedness from which no human efforts will probably deliver them. The fate of unborn Millions will now depend, under God, on the Courage and Conduct of this army—Our cruel and unrelenting Enemy leaves us no choice but a brave resistance, or the most abject submission; this is all we can expect—We have therefore to resolve to conquer or die: Our own Country's Honor, all call upon us for a vigorous and manly exertion, and if we now shamefully fail, we shall become infamous to the whole world—Let us therefore rely upon the goodness of the Cause, and the aid of the supreme Being, in whose hands Victory is, to animate and encourage us to great and noble Actions—The Eyes of all our Countrymen are now upon us, and we shall have their blessings, and praises, if happily we are the instruments of saving them from the Tyranny meditated against them. Let us therefore animate and encourage each other, and shew the whole world, that a Freeman contending for Liberty on his own ground is superior to any slavish mercenary on earth."[i]

~ from George Washington's General Orders to his men on July 2, 1776.

Preface

History is only boring to self-centered people. These people only care about events that have occurred in their lifetime. It's as though they believe that the world didn't really begin until they were born. What they don't seem to understand is that things that happened over two hundred years ago *do* have an effect on their lives.

I believe that everybody should learn about the experiences that previous generations went through in order to make a better future for us.

I put together this book because of the attempts being made to erase American history (especially the Founding). It's still being taught, but the whole story isn't being told. Instead it's being censored based on people's "feelings". Well I'm sorry, but you don't get to be offended by history. We study it for a reason, it's our roadmap for the future. Because history does repeat itself, and sometimes that's a good thing, but other times it's not. This is why I'm encouraging you to study history. Because if you don't, you won't recognize when something is going to happen again.

- Rebecca

Author's Note

All quotations in this book were copied verbatum. Any misspelled words or strange capitalization and punctuation were left uncorrected.

Table of Contents

1. A Search for Freedom..................1

2. How a Revolution is Born................6

3. The Shot Heard 'Round the World.........18

4. Appeal to Heaven....................23

5. The Declaration of Independence..........32

6. Fight for Freedom....................43

7. The Constitution of the United States of America..................................57

8. The Bill of Rights....................84

9. Jefferson's First Inaugural Address........89

10. Additional Amendments..........................98

11. A Necessary Evil..................................114

12. Freedom of the Press...........................121

13. Never Forget.......................................126

14. In God We Trust..................................129

Acknowledgements......................................140

About the Author..141

Index..142

Sources...150

Chapter 1
A Search for Freedom

Separation of Church and State

It doesn't mean what you've been taught to think it means.

~*~

English tyranny began with religion. This was the reason that the pilgrims came to America, to get out from under the Church of England and to seek a better life.

Holland was their first refuge. Their flight to the Netherlands during the reign of Elizabeth I was prompted by Parliament passing a law stating that should "any of her Majesty's subjects deny the Queen's ecclesiastical supremacy...they shall be committed to prison without bail".[1]

That, and one of their leaders, a Reverend John Greenwood, was executed in 1593 for "denying Her Majesty's ecclesiastical supremacy and attacking the existing ecclesiastical order", because he pointed out that "there could be but one head to the church and that head was not the Queen, but Christ".[2]

The Church of England was started in 1534 by King Henry VIII because he wanted to divorce Katherine of Aragon and marry Anne Boleyn (all because Katherine hadn't given him a male heir). The Catholic Church would not grant a divorce, so Henry created his own Church and set himself up as the head.[3]

When the pilgrims arrived in America they made sure to have separate leaders for the Church and for the State, because they believed that government had no right to "compel religion, to plant churches by power, and force a submission to ecclesiastical government by laws and penalties".[4]

That was the root of "separation of Church and State". It does not mean that God is taken out of the picture. It means that the State does not control the Church. This was pointed out many times by the early religious leaders. Here are just a couple examples:

"The separation of Church and State does not mean the exclusion of God, righteousness, morality, from the State". - Will Wood, a Quaker.[5]

"The separation of the Church from the State did not mean the severance of the State from God, or of the nation from Christianity". - Charles Galloway, a Methodist.[6]

The Bible makes it clear in 2 Chronicles 26, verses 16 through 21 that Church and State must remain separate. This is because the State will always try to control the Church, not the other way around.

~*~

Another religious sect that came to America in search of freedom were the Quakers.
In 1681 William Penn was given a large parcel of land by King Charles II as payment for a debt owed to Penn's late father. With it, Penn decided to form the colony of Pennsylvania in the New World for those seeking escape from religious persecution.
Penn himself was thrown in the Tower of London a total of four times for publicly stating

his beliefs. One of those times, in 1670, he was preaching outside becase the doors of the Quaker meeting house had been padlocked by the authorities. So they had him arrested and charged with "inciting a riot". Yeah, you've really gotta watch out for those violent Quakers...[7]

The Great Awakening

Despite America's Christian beginnings sometime between 1620 and 1734, faith had been allowed to fall by the wayside. This prompted men like Jonathan Edwards and George Whitfield to preach to the masses and remind them that God was still there. And thus began a spiritual revival that spread throughout the colonies over the next thirty-some years, and came to be known as the "Great Awakening".[8]

Ironically, George Whitfield was British. I say that it's ironic because there are historians who believe that this movement he helped to start actually played a key role in America's desire to break free from Great Britain.[9] Because, as it says in verse 1 of Galatians chapter 5:

"For freedom Christ has set us free; stand firm therefore, and do not submit again to a yoke of slavery."

The Seeds of Liberty

Nearly 150 years after the pilgrims came to America, Benjamin Franklin wrote to a judge in Scotland named Henry Home. The letter, dated February 25, 1767, contained a warning about the consequences of Great Britain's treatment of the American colonies:

"But America, an immense Territory, favour'd by Nature with all Advantages of Climate, Soil, great navigable Rivers and Lakes, &c. must become a great Country, populous and mighty; and will in a less time than is generally conceiv'd be able to shake off any Shackles that may be impos'd on her, and perhaps place them on the Imposers. In the mean time, every Act of Oppression will sour their Tempers, lessen greatly if not annihilate the Profits of your Commerce with them, and hasten their final Revolt: For the Seeds of Liberty are universally sown there, and nothing can eradicate them. And yet there remains among that People so much Respect, Veneration and Affection for Britain, that, if cultivated prudently, with kind Usage and Tenderness for their Privileges, they might be easily govern'd still for Ages, without Force or any considerable Expence. But I do not see here a sufficient Quantity of the Wisdom that is necessary to produce such a Conduct, and I lament the Want of it."[10]

Chapter 2
How a Revolution is Born

A storm was brewing in America.

"Taxation without representation!" was the cry throughout the colonies (mostly in Massachusetts) in 1765.[11]

An Essential Ingredient

To understand colonists' anger about unfair taxes, we must first go back to 1733 when the Molasses Act was passed in an attempt to force Americans to stop getting cheaper molasses and sugar from the French West Indies. The act said that six cents must be paid for every gallon of molasses that didn't come from a British held territory.[12]

But it wasn't really enforced and American smugglers just found ways around the law, so it didn't end up doing the British any good. Which is why Parliament repackaged it thirty-one years later as the 1764 Sugar Act. This act actually lowered the tax from six cents to three, but the money was put entirely towards keeping a standing army in the colonies. And this time the law *was* enforced.[13]

Many years later, in 1818, John Adams would write that "molasses was an essential ingredient in American independence".[14]

The Effects of the Stamp Act

The act required colonists to pay a one penny tax on *anything* that used paper[15] (equivalent to about $0.56 in 2021[16]).

These new taxes were meant to help alleviate Britain's debt aquired during the Seven Years' War (also known as the French and Indian War) which ended in 1763. And since that war had been fought in the colonies and was fought supposedly to protect the colonists from the

French, the British Parliament reasoned that the colonists should be the ones to pay for the war.[17]

Patrick Henry made a series of resolutions at Virginia's House of Burgesses that denied Parliament's right to tax the colonies on the grounds that the colonies had no representatives in Parliament. He also called for resistance of the Stamp Act. The resolutions were printed in newspapers throughout the colonies.[18]

In October of 1765 representatives from nine colonies formed the Stamp Act Congress and wrote to King George III saying that while they were loyal to him, they also believed that only colonial legislators had the authority to levy taxes.[19]

Meanwhile in Boston, the Sons of Liberty formed in protest of the tax and hung the effigy of the stamp distributor, Andrew Oliver, from a branch of the Liberty Tree before breaking into his home. Mr. Oliver then resigned his commission.[20]

Similar events occurred in other towns and by the beginning of 1766 most stamp distributors had resigned. And in port towns mobs prevented ships carrying stamp papers from unloading their cargo.[21]

Parliament eventually repealed the Stamp Act, however they passed more legislation at the same time, called the Declaratory Act. This act insisted that Parliament *did* have the power to pass any laws they wanted over the colonies.[22]

Not all members of Parliament felt superior to the colonists. One such man was William Pitt (soon to be Prime Minister) who said in a speech on January 14, 1766:
"I rejoice that America has resisted. Three million of people so dead to all feelings of liberty, as voluntarily to submit to be slaves, would have been fit instruments to make slaves of the rest."[23]

But Parliament did not listen to Pitt.

The Townshend Acts

Passed in 1767, they placed taxes on china, glass, lead, paint, paper and tea (all imported from Britain, naturally).[24]

The idea was that the money raised by these taxes would go towards paying the colonial governors and judges in order to keep them in the King's pocket.[25]

The plan backfired. Several towns in

Massachusetts, Connecticut and Rhode Island began boycotting British goods in January of 1768. New York followed their example in April. And it was suggested by Benjamin Franklin that the colonies should begin manufacturing their own goods.[26]

Parliament's response was to send more than 2,000 troops to occupy Boston.[27]

Needless to say, not everybody was happy about the military occupation.

The Boston Massacre

On the night of March 5, 1770 a mob formed around a lone British sentry in front of the Custom House on King Street and proceeded to verbaly abuse him. His commanding officer and seven of his fellow soldiers came to support him, at which point some members of the mob began throwing chunks of ice and taunting the soldiers to fire. In the ensuing confusion some of the soldiers did fire into the crowd, killing three men and wounding eight others, two of whom later died.[28]

People already hated British authorities and

this incident only added fuel to the fire.[29]

More than four years later, John Adams wrote this to a friend on December 28, 1774:
"The Death of 4 or 5 Persons, the most obscure, and inconsiderable that could have been found upon the Continent, on the 5th March 1770 has never yet been forgiven by any Part of America."[30]

The Tea Act

A month after the Boston Massacre all of the taxes were repealed, except for the tea tax.[31]

So, the colonists took to drinking smuggled Dutch tea instead.[32]

As a result, the East India Company began to go under. And Parliament couldn't have that, seeing as the Company was a big part of England's economy. So on May 10, 1773 they passed the Tea Act in an attempt to bail out the private company. The act gave the East India Company sole rights to sell their tea directly to the colonists, effectively cutting out colonial merchants.[33]

In retaliation, patriot groups convinced Company agents to quit their jobs. They also prevented Company ships from unloading their tea.[34]

But Massachusetts Royal Governor Thomas Hutchinson would not allow the tea ships to be turned back to England, insisting that they must be unloaded in Boston.[35]

So they were.

The Boston Tea Party

On the night of December 16, 1773, a large group of men "disguised" as Indians boarded the three East India Company ships anchored in Boston Harbor, the *Dartmouth*, the *Beaver* and the *Eleanor*, and proceeded to make the world's largest pot of tea by breaking open the tea chests and chucking them into the harbor. How's that for unloading?[36]

Here is an eyewitness account of the event by a man named Robert Sessions:

"I was living in Boston at the time, in the family of a Mr. Davis, a lumber merchant, as a common laborer. On that eventful evening, when Mr. Davis came in from the town meeting, I asked him what was to be done with the tea.

"They are now throwing it overboard," he replied.

"Receiving permission, I went immediately to the spot. Everything was as light as day, by means of lamps and torches—a pin might be seen lying on the wharf. I went on board where they were at work, and took hold with my own hands.

"I was not one of those appointed to destroy the tea, and who disguised themselves as Indians, but was a volunteer, the disguised men being largely men of family and position in Boston, while I was a young man whose home and relations were in Connecticut. The appointed and disguised party proving too small for the quick work necessary, other young men, similarly circumstanced with myself, joined them in their labors.

"The chests were drawn up by a tackle—one man bringing them forward in the hold, another putting a rope around them, and others hoisting them to the deck and carrying them to the vessel's side. The chests were then opened, the tea emptied over the side, and the chests thrown overboard.

"Perfect regularity prevailed during the whole transaction. Although there were many people on the wharf, entire silence prevailed—no clamor, no talking. Nothing was meddled with but the teas on board.

"After having emptied the hold, the deck was swept clean, and everything put in its proper place. An officer on board was requested to come up from the cabin and see that no damage was done except to the tea."[37]

This was not a group of hooligans throwing a temper tantrum, these men didn't set fire to the ships and make off with merchandise for themselves. Their only aim was to make a point about unfair taxes.

The day after the "Party", John Adams wrote this in his diary:
"Last Night 3 Cargoes of Bohea Tea were emptied into the Sea. This Morning a Man of War sails.
"This is the most magnificet Movement of all. There is a Dignity, a Majesty, a Sublimity, in this last Effort of the Patriots, that I greatly admire. The People should never rise, without doing something to be remembered—something notable And striking. This Destruction of the Tea is so bold, so daring, so firm, intrepid and inflexible, and it must have so important Consequences, and so lasting, that I cant but consider it as an Epocha in History."[38]

The Boston Port Act

As punishment, Parliament passed this act on March 30, 1774, closing the port of Boston until the colonists paid for the damage. The act also moved the seat of government to Salem and made Marblehead the main port of Massachusetts. Bostonians were furious that the entire city was being punished for the actions of just a few men.[39]

But the other colonies rallied to support them and sent supplies to the city by land.[40]

The Massachusetts Government Act

Passed on May 20, 1774, this act changed most elected officials to crown appointed.[41]

The Administration of Justice Act

Passed the same day as the Government Act, this act made it possible for royal officials accused of a crime to ask that their trial be held in a different colony or even in England.[42]

The Quartering Act
The Quartering Act of 1774 provided for British soldiers to be housed anywhere except in private homes.[43]

The First Continental Congress
The intention of these acts was to make an example of Massachusetts to the other colonies. As usual, Parliament's plan backfired.[44]

The First Continental Congress met in Philadelphia on September 5 of that year, the other colonies agreeing to unite with Massachusetts against Britain.[45]

"Give Me Liberty Or Give Me Death!"
Six and a half months later, on March 23, 1775 Patrick Henry made a passionate speech to the Virginia Convention:

"Should I keep back my opinions at such a time,...I should consider myself as guilty of treason toward my country, and of an act of disloyalty toward the Majesty of Heaven, which I revere above all earthly kings. We are not weak if we make proper use of those means which the God of nature hath placed in our power. Three million of people, armed in the holy cause of liberty, and in such a country as that we possess, are invincible by any force which our enemy can send us. Besides, sirs, we shall not fight our battles alone. There is a just God who presides over the destinies of nations, and who will raise up friends to fight our battles for us. The battle, sir, is not to the strong alone; it is to the vigilant, the active, the brave.

"Gentlemen may cry, Peace, Peace—but there is no peace. The war is actually begun!...Our brethren are already on the field! Why stand we here idle?... Is life so dear, or peace so sweet, as to be purchased at the price of chains and slavery? Forbid it, Almighty God! I know not what course others may take; but as for me, give me liberty or give me death!"[46]

Less than a month later British regulars would clash with Patriot minutemen on Lexington Common in Massachusetts, officially starting America's War for Independence.

Chapter 3
The Shot Heard 'Round the World

The American Revolution began in earnest on April 19, 1775, when British troops marched on the Massachusetts town of Concord with the intent of confiscating stores of powder. The town of Lexington lay enroute to Concord, and the militia had been warned about the approaching threat the night before by Paul Revere.[47]

Six days later, the captain of the militia would write this statement, claiming that the British fired first:

"I, John Parker, of lawful age, and commander of the Militia in Lexington, do testify and declare, that on the nineteenth instant, in the morning, about one of the clock, being informed that there were a number of Regular Officers riding up and down the road, stopping and insulting people as they passed the road, and also was informed that a number of Regular Troops were on their march from Boston, in order to take the Province Stores at Concord, ordered our militia to meet on the common in said Lexington, to consult what to do, and concluded not to be discovered, nor meddle or make with said Regular Troops (if they should approach) unless they should insult us; and upon their sudden approach, I immediately ordered our Militia to disperse and not to fire. Immediately said Troops made their appearance and rushed furiously, fired upon and killed eight of our party, with out receiving any provocation therefor from us."[48]

That makes it sound like the whole thing went down in the middle of the night, but it was actually dawn when the British showed up.[49]

Here is another account of the Battle of Lexington by a minuteman named Sylvannus Wood, who also claims that the British fired first:
"I immediately arose, took my gun, and with Robert Douglass went in haste to Lexington. When I arrived there, I inquired of Captain Parker the news. Parker told me he did not know what to

believe, for a man had come up about half an hour before and informed him that the British troops were not on the road. But while we were talking, a messenger came up and told the captain that the British troops were within half a mile. Parker immediately turned to his drummer, and ordered him to beat to arms....

"The British troops approached us rapidly in platoons, with a general officer on horseback at their head. The officer came up to within about two rods of the center of the company where I stood, the first platoon being about three rods distant. There they halted. The officer then swung his sword, and said, "Lay down your arms, you damned rebels, or you are all dead men— Fire!" Some guns were fired by the British at us from the first platoon, but no person was killed or hurt, being probably charged only with powder.

"Just at this time, Captain Parker ordered every man to take care of himself. The company immediately dispersed; and while the company was dispersing and leaping over the wall, the second platoon of the British fired, and killed some of our men. There was not a gun fired by any of Captain Parker's company, within my knowledge. I was so situated that I must have known it, had anything of the kind taken place before a total dispersion of our company. I have been intimately acquainted with the inhabitants of Lexington, and particularly with those of Captain Parker's company, and on one occasion, and with one exception, I have never heard any of them say or pretend that there was any firing at the British from Parker's company, or any individual in it....One member of the company told me, many years since, that, after Parker's company had dispersed, and he was at some distance, he gave them "the guts of his gun."[50]

There seems to be some confusion surrounding the "shot heard 'round the world" as it later came to be known. Parker and Wood both say that it came from the other side, with Wood specifically saying that a British officer *ordered* his men to fire.

On the other hand we have Major John Pitcairn (British) saying that he: "instantly called to the soldiers not to fire but to surround and disarm them". And a Lieutenant Sutherland who wrote that he: "heard Major Pitcairn's voice call out, 'Soldiers, don't fire, keep your ranks, form and surround them.'"[51]

Historians have simply thrown up their hands and said that we'll never know what really happened. And I don't think it matters too much. I'm grateful to whoever it was, British or

American, and I don't care if it was intentional or an accident. It needed to happen in order to really kick things off so that we could finally have it out with the British over our trampled rights.

Chapter 4
Appeal to Heaven

In 1775 America's first naval flag called for just that, because early Americans understood that only through God could they have victory over the most powerful empire on earth.

A Plea for Help
When some members of the Virginia legislature heard about the Boston Port Act they introduced a measure that called for a day of prayer and fasting, "devoutly to implore the Divine interposition in behalf of an injured and oppressed people."[52]
Included in this group of men were Thomas Jefferson, Richard Henry Lee, Francis Lightfoot Lee, and Patrick Henry.[53]

~*~

Reverend Jacob Duche', the Rector of Christ Church in Philadelphia, was asked to give the opening prayer for Congress on the morning of September 7, 1774. And after first reading from Psalms 35, this was what he prayed:

"O Lord our Heavenly Father, high and mighty King of kings and Lord of lords, who dost from Thy throne behold all the dwellers on earth and reignest with power supreme and uncontrolled over all the kingdoms, empires and governments; look down in mercy, we beseech Thee, on these our American States, who have fled to Thee from the rod of the oppressor and thrown themselves on Thy gracious protection, desiring to be henceforth dependent only on Thee. To Thee have they appealed for the righteousness of their cause; to Thee do they now look up for that countenance and support, which Thou alone canst give. Take them, therefore, Heavenly Father, under Thy nurturing care; give them wisdom in council and valor in the field; defeat the malicious designs of our cruel adversaries; convince them of the unrighteouness of their cause and if they persist in their sanguinary purposes, of own unerring justice, sounding in their hearts, constrain them to drop the weapons of war from their unnerved hands in the day of battle!

"Be Thou present, O God of wisdom, and direct the councils of this honorable assembly; enable them to settle things on the best and surest foundation. That the scene of blood may be speedily closed; that order, harmony, and peace may be effectually restored, and truth and justice, religion and piety, prevail and flourish amongst the people. Preserve the health of their bodies and vigor of their minds; shower down on them and the millions they here represent, such temporal blessings as Thou seest expedient for them in this world and crown them with everlasting glory in the world to come. All this we ask in the name and through the merits of Jesus Christ, Thy Son and our Savior.

"Amen."[54]

God Answers

On Long Island, New York, August 29, 1776, George Washington found his army outnumbered and soon to be surrounded. So he ordered a retreat. Most of the 9,000 troops were able to escape under cover of darkness. The remaining men, including Washington himself, were miraculously cloaked in a thick fog which descended on the river just as the sun was rising.[55]

Here is Lieutenant Benjamin Tallmadge's

account of the events:

"This was the first time in my life that I had witnessed the awful scene of a battle when man was engaged to destroy his fellowman. I well remember my sensations on the occasion, for they were solemn beyond description, and hardly could I bring my mind to be willing to attempt the life of a fellow creature. Our army having retired behind their entrenchment...the British army took their position in full array, directly in front of our position. Our entrenchment was so weak that it is most wonderful the British general did not attempt to storm it soon after the battle in which his troops had been victorious.

"General Washington was so fully aware of the perilous situation of this division of his army that he immediately convened a council of war, at which the propriety of retiring to New York was decided on. After sustaining incessant fatigue and constant watchfulness for two days and nights, attended by heavy rain, exposed every moment to an attack from a vastly superior force in front, and to be cut off from the possibility of a retreat to New York by the fleet which might enter the East River, on the night of the 29th of August General Washington commenced recrossing his troops from Brooklyn to New York.

"To move so large a body of troops, with all

their necessary appendages, across a river a full mile wide, with rapid current, in the face of a victorious, well-disciplined army nearly three times as numerous as his own, and a fleet capable of stopping the navigation so that not one boat could have passed over, seemed to present most formidable obstacles. But in face of these difficulties, the commander in chief so arranged his business that on the evening of the 29th, by 10 o'clock, the troops began to retire from the lines in such a manner that no chasm was made in the lines but as one regiment left their station on guard, the remaining troops moved to the right and left and filled up the vacancies, while General Washington took his station at the ferry and superintended the embarkation of the troops.

"It was one of the most anxious, busy nights that I ever recollect, and being the third in which hardly any of us had closed our eyes in sleep, we were all greatly fatigued. As the dawn of the next day approached, those of us who remained in the trenches became very anxious for our own safety, and when the dawn appeared there were several regiments still on duty. At this time a very dense fog began to rise, and it seemed to settle in a peculiar manner over both encampments. I recollect this peculiar providential occurence perfectly well; and so very dense was the atmosphere that I could scarcely discern a man at six yards' distance.

"When the sun rose we had just received orders to leave the lines, but before we reached the ferry, the commander in chief sent one of his aides to order the regiment to repair again to their former station on the lines. Colonel Chester immediately faced to the right about and returned, where we tarried until the sun had risen, but the fog remained as dense as ever. Finally, the second order arrived for the regiment to retire, and we very joyfully bid those trenches a long adieu. When we reached Brooklyn ferry, the boats had not returned from their last trip, but they very soon appeared and took the whole regiment over to New York; and I think I saw General Washington on the ferry stairs when I stepped into one of the last boats that received the troops."

Tallmadge concluded by saying:

"In the history of warfare I do not recollect a more fortunate retreat. After all, the providential appearance of the fog saved a part of our army from being captured, and certainly myself, among others who formed the rear guard."[56]

~*~

On October 10, 1780 the British held island of

Barbados was struck by the deadliest Atlantic hurricane in recorded history.[57] Meteorologists estimate that the winds were over 200mph.[58]

The forts on the island were destroyed and their cannons carried away.[59] And as for England's West Indies fleet, ten ships were wrecked, one sank, and seven others were damaged.[60]

Praise

The following song demonstrates the faith in God that those early Americans possessed. The song was written around 1778 by Boston church composer William Billings:

'Let tyrants shake their iron rod,
And slavery clank her galling chains,
We fear them not, we trust in God,
New England's God forever reigns.

Howe and Burgoyne and Clinton too,
With Prescott and Cornwallis join'd,
Together plot our overthrow,
In one infernal league combin'd.

When God inspir'd us for the fight,
Their ranks were broke, their lines were forc'd,
Their ships were shatter'd in our sight
Or swiftly driven from our coast.

The foe comes on with haughty stride,
Our troops advance with martial noise,
Their vet'rans flee before our youth,
And gen'rals yield to beardless boys.

What grateful offerings shall we bring?
What shall we render to the Lord?
Loud Hallelujahs let us sing,
And praise His name on ev'ry chord.'[61]

~*~

Near the end of the war, in May 1783, Ezra Stiles (a minister who helped found Brown University and was also a President of Yale)[62] made a speech to the General Assembly of Connecticut, refrencing God's obvious hand in the war:

"In our lowest and most dangerous state, in 1776 and 1777, we sustained ourselves against the British Army of sixty thousand troops, commanded by...the ablest generals Britain could procure throughout Europe, with a naval force of twenty-two thousand seamen in above eighty men-of-war.

"Who but a Washington, inspired by heaven, could have concieved the surprise move upon the enemy at Princeton—that Christmas eve when Washington and his army crossed the Delaware?

"Who but the Ruler of the winds could have delayed the British reinforcements by three months of contrary ocean winds at a critical point of the war?

"Or what but 'a providential miracle' at the last minute detected the treacherous scheme of traitor Benedict Arnold, which would have delivered the American army, including George Washington himself, into the hands of the enemy?

"On the French role in the Revolution, it is God who so ordered the balancing interests of nations as to produce an irresistable motive in the European maritime powers to take our part....

The United States are under peculiar obligations to become a holy people unto the Lord our God."[63]

We would do well to remember that.

Chapter 5
The Declaration of Independence

On June 7, 1776 a resolution of independence was introduced to the Second Continental Congress by Richard Henry Lee:

"Resolved

"That these United Colonies are, and of right ought to be, free and independent States, that they are absolved from all allegiance to the British Crown, and that all political connection between them and the State of Great Britain is, and ought to be, totally dissolved.

"That it is expedient forthwith to take the most effectual measures for forming foreign Alliances. That a plan of confederation be prepared and transmitted to the respective Colonies for their consideration and approbation."[64]

Four days later, on June 11, five men were appointed to a Declaration committee: John Adams (Massachusetts), Benjamin Franklin (Pennsylvania), Thomas Jefferson (Virginia), Robert Livingston (New York), and Roger Sherman (Connecticut).[65]

Adams lobbied for Jefferson to be the one to draft the document, saying that Jefferson could write ten times better than he could.[66]

So, on June 28, Jefferson's Declaration was presented to Congress by the Committee, and was officially adopted on July 4, two days after Congress voted to adopt Lee's original resolution.[67]

In the end it was not the same document that Jefferson had labored over for more than two weeks. Everybody had to put their two cents in during the debates, and some changes were made. The final result was the document that we know today:

When in the course of human events it becomes necessary for one people to dissolve the political bands which have connected them with another, and to assume among the powers of the earth, the seperate and equal station to which the Laws of Nature and of Nature's God entitle them, a decent respect to to the opinions of mankind requires that they should declare the causes which impel them to the separation.

We hold these truths to be self-evident, that all men are created equal, that they are endowed by their Creator with certain unalienable rights, that among these are Life, Libety, and the pursuit of Happiness. That to secure these rights, governments are instituted among men, deriving their just powers from the consent of the governed. That whenever any form of government becomes destructive of these ends, it is the right of the people to alter or to abolish it, and to institute new government, laying its foundation on such principles and organizing its powers in such form, as to them shall seem most likely to effect their safety and happiness. Prudence, indeed, will dictate that governments long established should not be changed for light and transient causes; and accordingly all experience hath shown, that mankind are more disposed to suffer, while evils are sufferable, than to right themselves by abolishing the forms to which they are accustomed. But when a long train of abuses and usurpations, pursuing invariably the same object, evinces a design to reduce them under absolute despotism, it is their right, it is their duty, to throw off such government, and to provide new guards for their future security. Such has been the patient sufferance of these Colonies; and such is now the necessity which constrains them to alter their former systems of government. The history of the present King of Great Britain is a history of repeated injuries and usurpations, all having, in direct object, the establishment of an absolute tyranny over these States. To prove this, let facts be submitted to a candid world.

He has refused his assent to laws, the most wholesome and necessary for the public good.

He has forbidden his Governors to pass laws of immediate and pressing importance, unless suspended in their operation till his assent should be obtained; and when so suspended, he has utterly neglected to attend to them.

He has refused to pass other laws for the accomodation of large districts of people, unless those people would relinquish the right of representation in the legislature, a right inestimable to them and formidable to tyrants only.

He has called together legislative bodies at places unusual, uncomfortable, and distant from the depository of their public records, for the sole purpose of fatiguing them into compliance with his measures.

He has dissolved representative houses repeatedly, for opposing with manly firmness his invasions on the rights of the people.

He has refused for a long time, after such dissolutions, to cause others to be elected; whereby the legislative powers, incapable of annihilation, have returned to the people at large for their exercise; the State remaining in the meantime exposed to all the dangers of invasion from without and convulsions within.

He has endeavoured to prevent the population of these states; for that purpose obstructing the laws of naturalization of foreigners; refusing to pass others to encourage their migration hither, and raising the conditions of new appropriations of lands.

He has obstructed the administration of justice, by refusing his assent to laws for establishing judiciary powers.

He has made judges dependent on his will alone, for the tenure of their offices, and the amount and payment of their salaries.

He has erected a multitude of new offices, and sent hither swarms of officers to harass our people, and eat out their substance.

He has kept among us, in times of peace, standing armies without the consent of our legislatures.

He has affected to render the military independent of, and superior to, the civil power.

He has combined with others to subject us to a jurisdiction foreign to our constitution, and unacknowledged by our laws; giving his assent to their acts of pretended legislation:

For quartering large bodies of armed troops among us:

For protecting them, by a mock trial, from punishment for any murders which they should commit on the inhabitants of these States:

For cutting off our trade with all parts of the world:

For imposing taxes on us without our consent:

For depriving us, in many cases, of the benefits of trial by jury:

For transporting us beyond seas to be tried for pretended offences:

For abolishing the free system of English laws in a neighboring Province, establishing therin an arbitrary government, and enlarging its boundaries so as to render it at once an example and fit instrument for introducing the same absolute rule into these Colonies:

For taking away our Charters, aboloshing our most valuable laws, and altering fundamentally the forms of our governments:

For suspending our own legislatures, and

declaring themselves invested with power to legislate for us in all cases whatsoever.

He has abdicated government here, by declaring us out of his protection and waging war against us.

He has plundered our seas, ravaged our coasts, burnt our towns, and destroyed the lives of our people.

He is, at this time, transporting large armies of foreign mercenaries to complete the works of death, desolation and tyranny, already begun, with circumstances of cruelty and perfidy scarcely paralleled in the most barbarous ages, and totally unworthy the head of a civilized nation.

He has constrained our fellow citizens taken captive on the high seas to bear arms against their country, to become the executioners of their friends and brethren, or to fall themselves by their hands.

He has excited domestic insurrections amongst us, and has endeavoured to bring on the inhabitants of our frontiers, the merciless Indian savages, whose known rule of warfare is an undistinguished destruction of all ages, sexes, and conditions.

In every stage of these oppressions we have petitioned for redress in the most humble terms: our repeated petitions have been answered only by repeated injury. A prince whose character is thus marked by every act which may define a tyrant is unfit to be the ruler of a free people.

Nor have we been wanting in attention to our British brethren. We have warned them from time to time of attempts by their legislature to extend an unwarrantable jurisdiction over us. We have reminded them of the circumstances of our emigration and settlement here. We have appealed to their native justice and magnanimity, and we have conjured them by the ties of our common kindred to disavow these usurpations, which would inevitably interrupt our connections and consanguinity. We must, therefore, aquiesce in the necessity, which denounces our seperation, and hold them, as we hold the rest of mankind, enemies in war, in peace, friends.

We, therefore, the Representatives of the United States of America, in General Congress assembled, appealing to the Supreme Judge of the world for the rectitude of our intentions, do, in the name, and by authority of the good people of these Colonies, solemnly publish and declare, That these United Colonies are, and of right ought to be, Free and Independent States; that they are absolved from all allegience to the British Crown, and that all political connection between them and the State of Great Britain, is and ought to be totally dissolved; and that as Free and Independent States, they have full power to levy war, conclude peace, contract alliances, establish commerce, and to do all other acts and things which Independent States may of right do. And for the support of this declaration, with a firm reliance on the protection of Divine Providence, we mutually pledge to each other our lives, our fortunes, and our sacred honor.

~*~

Jefferson would later write that the purpose of the Declaration was "to place before mankind the common sense of the subject; [in] terms so plain and firm, as to command their assent, and to justify ourselves in the independant stand we [were] compelled to take. Neither aiming at originality of principle or sentiment, nor yet copied from any particular and previous writing, it was intended to be an expression of the american mind, and to give to that expression the proper tone and spirit called for by the occasion".[68]

On July 1, the day before the Congress was to vote on independence, John Adams wrote this to Samuel Chase (Maryland):

"If you imagine that I expect this Declaration, will ward off, Calamities from this Country, you are much mistaken. A bloody Conflict We are destined to endure. This has been my opinion, from the Beginning. You will certainly remember, my decided opinion was, at the first Congress, when

We found, that We could not agree upon an immediate Non Exportation, that the Contest, would not be Settled without Bloodshed, and that, if Hostilities Should once commence, they would terminate in an incurable Animosity, between the two Countries. Every political Event, Since the Nineteenth of April 1775 has confirmed me in this opinion. If you imagine that I flatter myself, with Happiness and Halcyon days, after a Seperation from Great Britain, you are mistaken again. I dont expect that our new Governments will be So quiet, as I could wish, nor that happy Harmony, Confidence and Affection between the Colonies, that every good American ought to study, labor, and pray for, a long time."[69]

John Adams wrote to his wife, Abigail, from Philadelphia on July 3, 1776, reguarding Congress adopting the resolution for independence the day before:

"The Second Day of July 1776, will be the most memorable Epocha, in the History of America.—I am apt to believe that it will be celebrated, by succeeding Generations, as the great anniversary Festival. It ought to be commemorated, as the Day of Deliverance by solemn Acts of Devotion to God Almighty. It ought to be solemnized with Pomp and Parade, with Shews, Games, Sports, Guns, Bells,

Bonfires and Illuminations from one End of this Continent to the other from this Time forward forever more.

"You will think me transported with Enthusiasm but I am not.—I am well aware of the Toil and Blood and Treasure, that it will cost Us to maintain this Declaration, and support and defend these States.—Yet through all the Gloom I can see the Rays of ravishing Light and Glory. I can see that the End is more than worth all the Means. And that Posterity will tryumph in that Days Transaction, even altho We should rue it, which I trust in God We shall not."[70]

He was right, of course. Except for the date. Instead we celebrate the date that the Declaration itself was officially adopted.

~*~

The English were outraged when the Declaration finally made it into their newspapers. They considered it to be a treasonous document. Admiral Howe's secretary said that it proclaimed the "villany and madness of these deluded people".[71]

I guess that's sort of like being called "deplorables", or, "rubes"?

Chapter 6
Fight for Freedom

"No King but King Jesus"[72], became a common saying during the Revolution, as did this phrase from verse 29 of Acts chapter 5[73]:
"We must obey God rather than men."

~*~

In 1775, Boston was occupied by British forces, and under siege by the Continental Army. The following is an October 27th journal entry by one Timothy Newell:
"The spacious Old South Meeting House taken possession of by the Light Horse 17th Regiment of [British] Dragoons commanded by Lieutenant Colonel Samuel Birch. The pulpit, pews, and seats all cut to pieces and carried off in the most savage manner as can be expressed, and destined for a

riding school. The beautiful carved pew with the silk furniture of Deacon Hubbard's was taken down and carried to -------'s house by an officer and made a hog sty. The above was effected by a solicitation of General Burgoyne."[74]

~*~

There is a story about a preacher called John Muhlenburg preaching a sermon early in the war. According to the story the sermon was from Ecclesiastes 3:1, which says, "For everything there is a season, and a time for every matter under heaven". Then at the end he supposedly said, "In the language of the Holy Writ, there is a time for all things. There is a time to preach and a time to fight. And now is the time to fight", and then he revealed to the congregation that he was wearing his Continental Army Officer uniform under his clerical robes.[75]

This story may be just a legend, or it might be true, but the Bible *does* say in Ecclesiastes 3:8, that there is "a time for war, and a time for peace".

~*~

Excerpt from Thomas Paine's *Common Sense*,

published January 9, 1776:

"Alas! We have been long led away by ancient predjudices and made large sacrifices to superstition. We have boasted the protection of Great Britain, without considering that her motive was interest, not attachment, and that she did not protect us from our enemies on our account, but from her enemies on her own account....

"But Britain is the parent country say some. Then the more shame upon her conduct. Even brutes do not devour their young, nor savages make war upon their families....Europe and not England is the parent country of America. This New World has been the asylum for the persecuted lovers of civil and religious liberty from every part of Europe. Hither have they fled, not from the tender embraces of the mother, but from the cruelty of the monster; and it is so far true of England that the same tyranny which drove the first emigrants from home pursues their descendants still....

"It is not in the power of Britain to do this continent justice; the business of it will soon be too weighty and intricate to be managed with any tolerable degree of convenience, by a power so distant from us, and so very ignorant of us; for if they cannot conquer us, they cannot govern us. To be always running three or four thousand miles with a tale or a petition, waiting four or five months for an answer, which when obtained requires five or six more to explain it in, will in a few years be looked upon as folly and childishness—There was a time when it was proper, and there is a proper time for it to cease...

"America is only a secondary object in the system of British politics. England consults the good of this country no further than it answers her own purpose. Wherefore, her own interest leads her to suppress the growth of ours in every case which doth not promote her advantage, or in the least interferes with it....

"It is unreasonable to suppose that France or Spain will give us any kind of assistance, if we mean only to make use of that assistance for the purpose of repairing the breach and strengthening the connection between Britain and America; because, those powers would be sufferes by the consequences.

"While we profess ourselves the subjects of Britain, we must, in the eyes of foreign nations, be considered as Rebels....

"Were a manifest to be published and despatched to foreign courts, setting forth the miseries we have endured, and the peaceful methods which we have ineffectually used for redress....at the same time, assuring all such courts of our peaceable disposition towards them, and of our desire of entering into trade with them; such a memorial would produce more good effects to this continent than if a ship were freighted with petitions to Britain."[76]

~*~

When the national seal was being created in 1776, one of the mottos proposed was, "Rebellion to Tyrants is Obedience to God". Obviously this one wasn't the one they ended up using nationally, but in 1780 Thomas Jefferson had it put on the official state medal of Virginia while he was serving as governor.[77]

~*~

The following is an exerpt from a July 13, 1776 letter that Mary Bartlett wrote to her husband Josiah (one of the New Hampshire delegates to the Second Continental Congress):

"I fear the smallpox will spread universally as Boston is shut up with it and people flocking in for inoculation....The times look dark and gloomy upon the account of the wars. I believe this year will decide the fate of America—which way it will turn God only knows. We must look to Him for direction and protection; Job said though He slay me yet I will trust in Him."[78]

~*~

"These are the times that try men's souls; the summer soldier and the sunshine patriot will, in this crisis, shrink from the service of his country; but he that stands it now, deserves the love and thanks of man and woman. Tyranny, like hell, is not easily conquered; yet we have this consolation with us, that the harder the conflict, the more glorious the triumph." - from Thomas Paine's *The American Crisis*, published on December 19, 1776.[79] George Washington ordered these words be read to his men as they were preparing to attack Trenton.[80]

~*~

In the early morning hours of December 26, 1776 General Washington crossed the Delaware River with 2,400 of his men. Their intent was to attack the 1,500 Hessians stationed at Trenton, New Jersey.

Washington had formed his plan based on information provided by John Honeyman, a spy who had passed himself off as a loyalist while in Trenton. From Honeyman, Washington learned that the Hessians were virtually unprepared, as their commander, Colonel Johann Rall, was overly confident about his men's ability to repel an attack.

After making the crossing, Washington and his men headed south until they got closer to Trenton. Here they split into divisions and quickly surrounded the Hessians on three sides, driving them out of town to the east. After Rall tried and failed to make a counterattack, his men were forced to surrender.

The only American casualties in the Battle of Trenton were four killed and eight wounded.[81]

~*~

A Sergeant whose name has been lost to history, left this account of an event that transpired about a week after the Battle of Trenton:

"While we were at Trenton, on the last day of December, 1776, the time for which I and most of my regiment had enlisted expired. At this trying time General Washington, having now but a little handful of men, and many of them new recruits in which he could place little confidence, ordered our regiment to be paraded, and personally addressed us, urging that we should stay a month longer. He alluded to our recent victory at Trenton, told us that our services were greatly needed, and that we could now do more for our country than we ever could at any future period, and in the most affectionate manner entreated us to stay. The drums beat for volunteers, but not a man turned out. The soldiers, worn down by fatigue and privations, had their hearts fixed on home and the comforts of the domestic circle, and it was hard to forgo the anicipated pleasures of the society of our dearest friends.

"The General wheeled his horse about, rode in front of the regiment, and addressing us again said, "My brave fellows, you have done all I asked you to do, and more than could reasonably be expected; but your country is at stake, your wives, your houses, and all that you hold dear. You have worn yourselves out with fatigues and hardships, but we know not how to spare you. If you will consent to stay only one month longer, you will render that service to the cause of liberty, and to your country, which you probably never can do under any other circumstances. The present is emphatically the crisis, which is to decide our destiny".

"The drums beat a second time. The soldiers felt the force of the appeal. One said to another, "I will remain if you will." Others remarked, "We cannot go home under such circumstances." A few stepped forth, and their example was immediately followed by nearly all who were fit for duty in the regiment, amounting to about two hundred volunteers."[82]

THE SPIRIT OF AMERICA

~*~

King George III made a typically arrogant address to Parliament on November 18, 1777:

"I still hope that the deluded and unhappy multitude will return to their allegiance. And that the remembrance of what they once enjoyed, the regret for what they lost, and the feelings of what they now suffer under the arbitrary tyranny of their leaders will rekindle in their hearts a spirit of loyalty to their sovereign, and a spirit of loyalty to their mother country."[83]

Because calling your subjects stupid is definitely going to make them want to come back...

And saying that the colonial leadership was tyrannical? Wow, talk about projection.

William Pitt had a very different view, which he proclaimed after the King was through speaking:

"I rise, my Lords, to declare my sentiments on this most solemn and serious subject....I love and honor the English troops. I know their virtues and their valor. I know they can achieve anything except impossibilities. And I know that the conquest of English America is an impossibility.

"My Lords, you can not conquer America. What is your present situation there? We do not know the worst, but we know that in three campaigns we have done nothing and suffered much. Besides the sufferings, perhaps total loss of the Northern force, the best appointed army that ever took the field, commanded by Sir William Howe, has retired from the American lines....

"As to conquest, therefore, my Lords, I repeat, it is impossible. You may swell every expense and every effort still more extravagantly, pile and accumulate every assistance you can buy or borrow, traffic and barter with every little pitiful German prince that sells and sends his subjects to the shambles of a foreign prince—your efforts are forever vain and impotent. If I were an American, as I am an Englishman, while a foreign troop was landed in my country, I never would lay down my arms.

"Never. Never. Never.

"I call upon the spirit and humanity of my country, to vindicate the national character. I invoke the genius of the Constitution. From the tapestry that adorns these walls, the immortal ancestor of this noble Lord frowns with indignation at the disgrace of his country."[84]

~*~

In an attempt to end the war, Parliament passed the Taxation of the Colonies Act in 1778. The act stated that Parliament would no longer tax the colonies because it had "been found by experience to occasion great uneasiness and disorders".[85]

No, really?

~*~

Just weeks before the surrender at Yorktown, Benedict Arnold, now a British General, led a raid on New London, Connecticut. And all the American soldiers who surrendered were immediately killed. You see, the British thought the Americans were lowly traitors, so killing them was justified. As one British officer wrote about a different battle:

"The Hessians and brave Highlanders gave no quarters, and it was a fine sight to see with what alacrity they dispatched the rebels with their bayonets after we had surrounded them so they could not resist."[86]

This comes from a citizen of the so-called great civilized nation of England.

~*~

Colonel Benjamin Tallmadge described the scene of George Washington saying goodbye to his officers in Fraunces Tavern on Pearl Street in New York City at the end of the war:

"We had been assembled but a few moments when His Excellency entered the room. His emotion, too strong to be concealed, seemed to be reciprocated by every officer present.

"After partaking of a slight refreshment, in almost breathless silence, the general filled his glass with wine, and turning to his officers, he said, "With a heart full of gratitude, I now take leave of you. I most devoutly wish that your latter days may be as prosperous and happy as your former days have been glorious and honorable."

"After the officers had taken a glass of wine, General Washington said, "I cannot come to each of you, but shall feel obligated if each of you will come and take me by the hand."

"General Knox, being nearest to him, turned to the commander in chief, who, suffused in tears, was incapable of utterance, but grasped his hand, when they embraced each other in silence."

Tallmadge continued:

"Such a scene of sorrow and weeping I had

never before witnessed, and hope I may never be called upon to witness again....Not a word was uttered to break the solemn silence...or to interrupt the tenderness of the...scene. The simple thought that we were then about to part from the man who had conducted us through a long and bloody war, and under whose conduct the glory and independence of our country had been achieved, and that we should see his face no more in this world, seemed to me utterly insupportable.

"But the time of separation had come, and waving his hand to his grieving children around him, he left the room, and passing through a corps of light infantry who were paraded to receive him, he walked silently on to Whitehall, where a barge was in waiting. We all followed in mournful silence to the wharf, where a prodigious crowd had assembled to witness the departure of the man who, under God, had been the great agent in establishing the glory and and independence of these United States. As soon as he was seated, the barge put off into the river, and when out in the stream, our great and beloved General waved his hat and bid us a silent adieu."[87]

~*~

It is believed that around 376,000 Americans

fought in the Revolution and that roughly 23,800 of that number perished during the war. The majority of fatalities were caused by various diseases with the death toll estimated to be 5,000 to 9,000. It is thought that as many as 20,000 were taken prisoner, and anywhere from 8,000 to 12,000 of them died because of inhumane conditions, mostly on the British prison ships (HMS *Jersey* is a prime example). Deaths in battle made up the smallest percentage at just an estimated 6,800.[88]

However their lives were given, they were given for freedom. For the freedom of those born and unborn.

Chapter 7

The Constitution of the United States of America

Near the beginning of the Constitutional Convention in the summer of 1787, Benjamin Franklin had some advice to give. He spoke directly to George Washington (President of the Convention) but it was meant for all the delegates to hear:

"I have lived, sir, a long time, and the longer I live, the more convincing proofs I see of His truth, that God governs the affairs of men. And if a sparrow cannot fall to the ground without His notice, it is probable that an empire can rise without His aid? We have been assured, sir, in the Sacred Writings, that "except the Lord builds the house, they labor in vain that build it." I firmly believe this; and I also believe that without His concurring aid we shall suceed in this political building no better than the builders of Babel: We shall be divided by our partial local interests; our projects will be confounded, and we ourselves shall become a reproach and bye word down to future ages. And what is worse, mankind may hereafter from this unfortunate instance, despair of establishing governments by human wisdom and leave it to chance, war, and conquest.

"I therefore beg leave to move that henceforth prayers imploring the assistance of Heaven, and its blessings on our deliberations, be held in this assembly every morning before we proceed to business, and that one or more of the clergy of this city be requested to officiate in that service."[89]

~*~

The result of this convention was the following document:

We, the people of the United States, in order to form a more perfect union, establish justice, insure domestic tranquility, provide for the common defense, promote the general welfare, and secure the blessings of liberty to ourselves and our posterity, do ordain and establish this Constitution for the United States of America.

ARTICLE I

Section 1. All legislative powers herein granted shall be vested in a Congress of the United States, which shall consist of a Senate and House of Representatives.

Section 2. 1. The House of Representatives shall be composed of members chosen every second year by the people of the several States, and the electors in each State shall have the qualifications requisite for electors of the most numerous branch of the State legislature.

2. No person shall be a representative who shall not have attained to the age of twenty-five years, and been seven years a citizen of the United States, and who shall not, when elected, be an inhabitant of that State in which he shall be chosen.

3. Representatives and direct taxes shall be apportioned among the several States which may be included within this Union, according to their respective numbers, which shall be determined by adding to the whole number of free persons, including those bound to service for a term of years, and excluding Indians not taxed, *three fifths of all other persons*. The actual enumeration shall

be made within three years after the first meeting of the Congress of the United States, and within every subsequent term of ten years, in such manner as they shall by law direct. The number of representatives shall not exceed one for every thirty thousand, but each State shall have at least one representative; and until such enumeration shall be made, the State of New Hampshire shall be entitled to choose three, Massachusetts eight, Rhode Island and Providence Plantations one, Connecticut five, New York six, New Jersey four, Pennsylvania eight, Delaware one, Maryland six, Virginia ten, North Carolina five, South Carolina five, and Georgia three.

4. When vacancies happen in the representation from any State, the executive authority thereof shall issue writs of election to fill such vacancies.

5. The House of Representatives shall choose their speaker and other officers; and shall have the sole power of impeachment.

Section 3. 1. The Senate of the United States shall be composed of two senators from each State, *chosen by the legislature thereof*, for six years; and each senator shall have one vote.

2. Immediately after they shall be assembled in consequence of the first election, they shall be divided as equally as may be into three classes. The seats of the senators of the first class shall be

vacated at the expiration of the second year, of the second class at the expiration of the fourth year, and the third class at the expiration of the sixth year, so that one third may be chosen every second year; and if vacancies happen by resignation, or otherwise, during the recess of the legislature of any State, the executive thereof may make temporary appointments until the next meeting of the legislature, which shall then fill such vacancies.

3. No person shall be a senator who shall not have attained to the age of thirty years, and been nine years a citizen of the United States, and who shall not, when elected, be an inhabitant of that State for which he shall be chosen.

4. The Vice-President of the United States shall be President of the Senate, but shall have no vote, unless they be equally divided.

5. The Senate shall choose their other officers, and also a president *pro tempore*, in the absence of the Vice-President, or when he shall exercise the office of the President of the United States.

6. The Senate shall have the sole power to try all impeachments. When sitting for that purpose, they shall be on oath or affirmation. When the President of the United States is tried, the chief justice shall preside: and no person shall be convicted without the concurrence of two thirds of the members present.

7. Judgment in cases of impeachment shall not extend further than to removal from office, and disqualifications to hold and enjoy any office of honor, trust or profit under the United States: but the party convicted shall nevertheless be liable and subject to indictment, trial, judgment and punishment, according to law.

Section 4. 1. The times, places, and manner of holding elections for senators and representatives, shall be prescribed in each state by the legislature thereof; but the Congress may at any time by law make or alter such regulations, except as to the places of choosing senators.

2. The Congress shall assemble at least once in every year, and such meeting shall be on the first Monday in December, unless they shall by law appoint a different day.

Section 5. 1. Each House shall be the judge of the elections, returns and qualifications of its own members, and a majority of each shall constitute a quorum to do business; but a smaller number may adjourn from day to day, and may be authorized to compel the attendance of absent members, in such manner, and under such penalties as each House may provide.

2. Each House may determine the rules of its proceedings, punish its members for disorderly behavior, and, with the concurrence of two thirds,

expel a member.

3. Each House shall keep a journal of its proceedings, and from time to time publish the same, excepting such parts as may in their judgment require secrecy; and the yeas and nays of the members of either House on any question shall, at the desire of one fifth of those present, be entered on the journal.

4. Neither House, during the session of Congress, shall, without the consent of the other, adjourn for more than three days, nor to any other place than that in which the two Houses shall be sitting.

Section 6. 1. The senators and representatives shall receive a compensation for their services, to be ascertained by law, and paid out of the Treasury of the United States. They shall in all cases, except treason, felony, and breach of the peace, be privileged from arrest during their attendance at the session of their respective Houses, and in going to and returning from the same; and for any speech or debate in either House, they shall not be questioned in any other place.

2. No senator or representative shall, during the time for which he was elected, be appointed to any civil office under the authority of the United States, which shall have been created, or the emoluments whereof shall have been increased during such

time; and no person holding any office under the United States shall be a member of either House during his continuance in office.

Section 7. 1. All bills for raising revenue shall originate in the House of Representatives; but the Senate may propose or concur with amendments as on other bills.

2. Every bill which shall have passed the House of Representatives and the Senate, shall, before it becomes a law, be presented to the President of the United States; if he approve he shall sign it, but if he shall return it, with his objections, to that House in which it shall have originated, who shall enter the objections at large on their journal, and proceed to reconsider it. If after such reconsideration two thirds of that House shall agree to pass the bill, it shall be sent, together with the objections, to the other House, by which it shall likewise be reconsidered, and if approved by two thirds of that House, it shall become a law. But in all such cases the votes of both Houses shall be determind by yeas and nays, and the names of the persons voting for and against the bill shall be entered into the journal of each House respectively. If any bill shall not be returned by the President within ten days (Sundays excepted) after it shall have been presented to him, the same shall be a law, in like manner as if he had signed it, unless the Congress by their adjournment

prevent its return, in which case it shall not be a law.

3. Every order, resolution, or vote to which the concurrence of the Senate and the House of Representatives may be necessary (except on a question of adjournment) shall be presented to the President of the United States; and before the same shall take effect, shall be approved by him, or being disapproved by him, shall be repassed by two thirds of the Senate and House of Representatives, according to the rules and limitations prescribed in the case of a bill.

Section 8. The Congress shall have the power

1. To lay and collect taxes, duties, imposts, and excises, to pay the debts and provide for the common defense and general welfare of the United States; but all duties, imposts, and excises shall be uniform throughout the United States;

2. To borrow money on the credit of the United States;

3. To regulate commerce with foreign nations, and among the several States, and with the Indian tribes;

4. To establish a uniform rule of naturalization, and uniform laws on the subject of bankruptcies throughout the United States;

5. To coin money, regulate the value thereof, and of foreign coin, and fix the standard of weights

and measures;

6. To provide for the punishment of counterfeiting the securities and current coin of the United States;

7. To establish post offices and post roads;

8. To promote the progress of science and useful arts, by securing for limited times to authors and inventors the exclusive right to their respective writings and discoveries;

9. To constitute tribunals inferior to the Supreme Court;

10. To define and punish piracies and felonies committed on the high seas, and offenses against the law of nations;

11. To declare war, grant letters of marque and reprisal, and make rules concerning captures on land and water;

12. To raise and support armies, but no appropriation of money to that use shall be for a longer term than two years;

13. To provide and maintain a navy;

14. To make rules for the government and regulation of the land and naval forces;

15. To provide for calling forth the militia to execute the laws of the Union, suppress insurrections and repel invasions;

16. To provide for organizing, armies, and disciplining the militia, and for governing such part

of them as may be employed in the service of the United States, reserving to the States respectively, the appointment of the officers, and the authority of training the militia according to the discipline prescribed by Congress;

17. To exercise exclusive legislation in all cases whatsoever, over such district (not exceeding ten miles square) as may, by cession of particular States, and the acceptance of Congress, become the seat of the government of the United States, and to exercise like authority over all places purchased by the consent of the legislature of the State in which the same shall be, for the erection of forts, magazines, arsenals, dockyards, and other needful buildings; and

18. To make all laws which shall be necessary and proper for carrying into execution the foregoing powers, and all other powers vested by this Constitution in the government of the United States, or in any department or officers thereof.

Section 9. 1. The migration or importation of such persons as any of the States now existing shall think proper to admit, shall not be prohibited by the Congress prior to the year one thousand eight hundred and eight, but a tax or duty may be imposed on such importation, not exceeding ten dollars for each person.

2. The privilege of the writ of *habeas corpus*

shall not be suspended, unless when in cases of rebellion or invasion the public safety may require it.

3. No bill of attainder or *ex post facto* law shall be passed.

4. No capitation, or other direct, tax shall be laid, unless in proportion to the census or enumeration hereinbefore directed to be taken.

5. No tax or duty shall be laid on articles exported from any State.

6. No preference shall be given by any regulation of commerce or revenue to the ports of one State over those of another: nor shall vessels bound to, or from, one State be obliged to enter, clear, or pay duties in another.

7. No money shall be drawn from the treasury, but in consequence of appropriations made by law; and a regular statement and account of the receipts and expenditures of all public money shall be published from time to time.

8. No title of nobility shall be granted by the United States: and no person holding any office of profit or trust under them, shall, without the consent of the Congress, accept of any present, emolument, office, or title, of any kind whatever, from any king, prince, or foreign State.

Section 10. 1. No State shall enter into any treaty, alliance, or confederation; grant letters of marque and reprisal; coin money; emit bills of credit; make anything but gold and silver coin a tender in payment of debts; pass any bill of attainder, *ex post facto* law, or law impairing the obligation of contracts, or grant any title of nobility.

2. No State shall, without the consent of the Congress, lay any imposts or duties on imports or exports, except what may be absolutely necessary for executing its inspection laws; and the net produce of all duties and imposts laid by any State on imports or exports, shall be for the use of the Treasury of the United States; and all such laws shall be subject to the revision and control of the Congress.

3. No State shall, without the consent of the Congress, lay any duty of tonnage, keep troops, or ships of war in time of peace, enter into any agreement or compact with another State, or with a foreign power, or engage in war, unless actually invaded, or in such imminent danger as will not admit of delay.

ARTICLE II

Section 1. 1. The executive power shall be vested in a President of the United States of America. He shall hold his office during the term of four years, and, together with the Vice President, chosen for the same term, be elected as follows:

2. Each State shall appoint, in such manner as the legislature thereof may direct, a number of electors, equal to the whole number of senators and representatives to which the State may be entitled in the Congress: but no senator or representative, or person holding an office of trust or profit under the United States, shall be appointed an elector.

The electors shall meet in their respective States, and vote by ballot for two persons, of whom one at least shall not be an inhabitant of the same State with themselves. And they shall make a list of all the persons voted for, and of the number of votes for each; which list they shall sign and certify, and transmit sealed to the seat of the government of the United States, directed to the President of the Senate. The President of the Senate shall, in the presence of the Senate and House of Representatives, open all the certificates, and the votes shall then be counted. The person having the greatest number of votes shall be the President, if such number be a majority of the whole number of electors appointed; and if there be more than one who have such majority, and have an equal number of votes, then the House of Representatives shall immediatly choose by ballot one of them for President; and if no person have a majority, then from the five highest on the list the said House shall in like manner choose the President. But in choosing the President, the votes shall be taken by States, the representation from each State having one vote; a quorum for this purpose shall consist of a member or members from two thirds of the States, and a majority of all the States shall be necessary to a choice. In every case, after the choice of the President, the person having the greatest number of votes of the electors shall be the Vice President. But if there should remain two or more who have equal votes, the Senate shall choose from them by ballot the Vice President.

3. The Congress may determine the time of choosing the electors, and the day on which they shall give their votes; which day shall be the same throughout the United States.

4. No person except a natural born citizen, or a citizen of the United States at the time of the adoption of this Constitution, shall be eligible to the office of President; neither shall any person be eligible to that office who shall not have attained to the age of thirty-five years, and been fourteen years a resident within the United States.

5. In case of the removal of the President from office, or of his death, resignation, or inability to discharge the powers and duties of the said office, the same shall devolve on the Vice President, and

the Congress may by law provide for the case of removal, death, resignation, or inability, both of the President and Vice President, declaring what officer shall then act as President, and such officer shall act accordingly, until the disability be removed, or a President shall be elected.

6. The President shall, at stated times, receive for his services a compensation, which shall neither be increased nor diminished during the period for which he shall have been elected, and he shall not receive within that period any other emolument from the United States, or any of them.

7. Before he enter the execution of his office, he shall take the following oath or affirmation:-"I do solemnly swear (or affirm) that I will faithfully execute the office of President of the United States, and will to the best of my ability, preserve, protect and defend the Constitution of the United States."

Section 2. 1. The President shall be Commander-in-chief of the Army and Navy of the United States, and of the militia of the several States, when called into the actual service of the United States; he may require the opinion, in writing, of the principal officer in each of the executive departments, upon any subject relating to the duties of their respective offices, and he shall have power to grant reprieves and pardons for offenses against the United States, except in cases of impeachment.

2. He shall have power, by and with the advice and consent of the Senate, to make treaties, provided two-thirds of the senators present concur; and he shall nominate, and by and with the advice and consent of the Senate, shall appoint ambassadors, other public ministers and consuls, judges of the Supreme Court, and all other officers of the United States, whose appointments are not herein otherwise provided for, and which shall be established by law: but the Congress may by law vest the appointment of such inferior officers, as they think proper, in the President alone, in the courts of law, or in the heads of departments.

3. The President shall have power to fill up all vacancies that may happen during the recess of the Senate, by granting commissions which shall expire at the end of their next session.

Section 3. He shall from time to time give to the Congress information of the state of the Union, and recommend to their consideration such measures as he shall judge necessary and expedient; he may, on extraordinary occasions, convene both Houses, or either of them, and in case of disagreement between them with respect to the time of adjournment, he may adjourn them to such time as he shall think proper; he shall receive ambassadors and other public ministers; he shall take care that the laws be faithfully executed, and shall commission all the officers of the United States.

Section 4. The President, Vice President, and all civil officers of the United States, shall be removed from office on impeachment for, and conviction of, treason, bribery, or other high crimes and misdemeanors.

ARTICLE III

Section 1. The judicial power of the United States shall be vested in one Supreme Court, and in such inferior courts as the Congress may from time to time ordain and establish. The judges, both of the Supreme and inferior courts, shall hold their offices during good behavior, and shall, at stated times, receive for their services, a compensation which shall not be diminished during their continuance in office.

Section 2. 1. The judicial power shall extend to all cases, in law and equity, arising under this Constitution, the laws of the United States, and treaties made, or which shall be made, under their authority;--to all cases affecting ambassadors, other public ministers and consuls;--to all cases of admiralty and maritime jurisdiction;--to controversies to which the United States shall be a party;--to controversies between two or more States;--between a State and citizens of another State;--between citizens of different States;--between citizens of the same State claiming lands under grants of different States, and between a State, or the citizens thereof, and foreign States, citizens or subjects.

2. In all cases affecting ambassadors, other public ministers and consuls, and those in which a State shall be party, the Supreme Court shall have original jurisdiction. In all the other cases before mentioned, the Supreme Court shall have appellate jurisdiction, both as to law and to fact, with such exceptions, and under such regulations as the Congress shall make.

3. The trial of all crimes, except in cases of impeachment, shall be by jury; and such trial shall be held in the State where the said crimes shall have been committed; but when not committed within any State, the trial shall be at such place or places as the Congress may by law have directed.

Section 3. 1. Treason against the United States shall consist only in levying war against them, or in adhering to their enemies, giving them aid and comfort. No person shall be convicted of treason unless on the testimony of two witnesses to the same overt act, or on confession in open court.

2. The Congress shall have power to declare the

punishment of treason, but no attainder of treason shall work corruption of blood, or forfeiture except during the life of the person attained.

ARTICLE IV

Section 1. Full faith and credit shall be given in each State to the public acts, records, and judicial proceedings of every other State. And the Congress may by general laws prescribe the manner in which such acts, records and proceedings shall be proved, and the effect thereof.

Section 2. 1. The citizens of each State shall be entitled to all privileges and immunities of citizens in the several States.

2. A person charged in any State with treason, felony, or other crime, who shall flee from justice, and be found in another State, shall, on demand of the executive authority of the State from which he fled, be delivered up to be removed to the State having jurisdiction of the crime.

3. No person held to service or labor in one State under the laws thereof, escaping into another, shall, in consequence of any law or regulation therein, be discharged from such service or labor, but shall be delivered up on claim of the party to whom such service or labor may be due.

Section 3. 1. New States may be admitted by the Congress into this Union; but no new State shall be formed or erected within the jurisdiction of any other State; nor any State be formed by the junction of two or more States, or parts of States, without the consent of the legislatures of the States concerned as well as of the Congress.

2. The Congress shall have power to dispose of and make all needful rules and regulations respecting the territory or other property belonging to the United States; and nothing in this Constitution shall be so constructed as to prejudice any claims of the United States, or of any particular State.

Section 4. The United States shall guarantee to every State in this Union a republican form of government, and shall protect each of them against invasion; and on application of the legislature, or of the executive (when the legislature cannot be convened), against domestic violence.

ARTICLE V

The Congress, whenever two thirds of both Houses shall deem it necessary, shall propose amendments to this Constitution, or, on the application of the legislatures of two-thirds of the several States, shall call a convention for proposing amendments, which, in either case, shall be valid to all intents and purposes, as part of this Constitution, when ratified by the legislatures of three fourths of the several States, or by conventions in three fourths thereof, as the one or the other mode of ratification may be proposed by the Congress; Provided that no amendment which may be made prior to the year one thousand eight hundred and eight shall in any manner affect the first and fourth clauses in the ninth section of the first article; and that no State, without its consent, shall be deprived of its equal suffrage in the Senate.

ARTICLE VI

1. All debts contracted and engagements entered into, before the adoption of this Constitution, shall be as valid against the United States under this Constitution, as under the Confederation.

2. This Constitution, and the laws of the United States which shall be made in pursuance thereof, and all treaties made, or which shall be made, under the authority of the United States, shall be the supreme law of the land; and the Judges in every State shall be bound thereby, anything in the Constitution or laws of any State to the contrary

notwithstanding.

3. The senators and representatives before mentioned, and the members of the several States legislatures, and all executive and judicial officers, both of the United States and of the several States, shall be bound by oath or affirmation to support this Constitution; but no religious test shall ever be required as a qualification to any office or public trust under the United States.

ARTICLE VII

The ratification of the conventions of nine States shall be sufficient for the establishment of this Constitution between the States so ratifying the same.

~*~

Benjamin Franklin had this to say about the final draft of the Constitution on September 17, 1787 (the day it was signed):

"I confess that I do not entirely approve of this Constitution at present, but, Sir, I am not sure I shall never approve it: For having lived long, I have experienced many instances of being obliged, by better information or fuller consideration, to change opinions even on important subjects, which I once thought right, but found to be otherwise. It is therefore that the older I grow the more apt I am to doubt my own judgement, and to pay more respect to the judgement of others."

Franklin continued:

"In these sentiments, Sir, I agree to this Constitution, with all its faults, if they are such; because I think a general government necessary for us, and there is no form of government but what may be a blessing to the people if well administered; and I believe further that this is likely to be well administered for a course of years, and can only end in despotism, as other forms of have done before it, when the people shall become so corrupted as to need despotic government, being incapable of any other.

"I doubt, too, whether any other convention we can obtain may be able to make a better Constitution: for when you assemble a number of men to have the advantage of their joint wisdom, you inevitably assemble with those men all their predjudices, their passions, their errors of opinion, their local interests, and their selfish views. From such an assembly can a perfect production be expected? It therefore astonishes me, Sir, to find this system approaching so near to perfection as it does; and I think it will astonish our enemies, who are waiting with confidence to hear that our councils are confounded, like those of the builders of Babel, and that our states are on the point of separation, only to meet hereafter for the purpose of cutting one another's throats.

"Thus I consent, Sir, to this Constitution because I expect no better, and because I am not sure that it is not the best. The opinions I have had of its errors I sacrifice to the public good. I have never whispered a syllable of them abroad. Within these walls they were born, and here they shall die. If every one of us in returning to our constituents were to report the objections he has had to it, and use his influence to gain partisans in support of them, we might prevent its being generally received, and thereby lose all the salutary effects and great advantages resulting naturally in our favor among foreign nations, as well as among ourselves, from our real or apparent unanimity.

"Much of the strength and efficiency of any government, in procuring and securing happiness to the people depends on opinion, on the general opinion of the goodness of that government as well as of the wisdom and integrity of its governors. I hope, therefore, that for our own sakes, as a part of the people, and for the sake of our posterity, we shall act heartily and unanimously in recommeding this Constitution, wherever our influence may extend, and turn our future thoughts and endeavors to the means of having it well administered.

"On the whole, Sir, I cannot help expressing a wish that every member of the convention, who may still have objections to it, would with me on this occasion doubt a little of his own infallibility, and to make manifest our unanimity, put his name to this instrument."[90]

~*~

After the document had been signed a few of the delegates spoke of God's hand in the forming of our government:

Benjamin Franklin:

"To conclude, I beg I may not be understood to infer, that our General Convention was divinely inspired when it formed the new Federal Constitution,...yet I must own I have so much faith in the general government of the world by Providence, that I can hardly conceive a transaction of such momentous importance to the welfare of millions now existing, and to exist in the posterity of a great nation, should be suffered to pass without being in some degree influenced, guided, and governed by that omnipotent, omnipresent, and beneficent Ruler, in whom all inferior spirits live and move and have their being." [91]

Charles Pinckney (one of the South Carolina delegates):
"Nothing less than that superintending hand of Providence, that so miraculously carried us through war (in my humble opinion), could have brought it [the Constitution] about so complete, upon the whole."[92]

Alexander Hamilton:
"For my own part, I sincerely esteem it a system, which, without the finger of God, never could have been suggested and agreed upon by such a diversity of interests."[93]

George Washington wrote to the Marquis de Lafayette in February of 1788 that he thought it was, "little short of a miracle".[94]

There is no denying that God gave us this country. Are we so ungrateful that we will not fight to preserve it?

Chapter 8
The Bill of Rights

Our basic rights, without which we are lost.

ARTICLE I

Congress shall make no law respecting an establishment of religion, or prohibiting the free exercise thereof; or abridging the freedom of speech, or of the press; or the right of the people peaceably to assemble, and to petition the government for a redress of grievances.

~*~

This one evidently no longer applies.

ARTICLE II

A well regulated militia being necessary to the

security of a free State, the right of the people to keep and bear arms shall not be infringed.

~*~

This one is currently under attack.

"The strongest reason for the people to retain the right to bear arms is, as a last resort, to protect themselves against tyranny in government." - Thomas Jefferson[95]

"What is the militia? It is the whole people. To disarm the people is the best and most effective way to enslave them." - George Mason, one of the Virginia delegates at the Constitutional Convention. [96]

ARTICLE III

No soldier shall, in time of peace, be quartered in any house, without consent of the owner, nor in time of war, but in a manner to be prescribed by law.

ARTICLE IV

The right of the people to be secure in their persons, houses, papers, and effects, against unreasonable searches and seizures, shall not be violated, and no warrants shall issue, but upon probable cause, supported by oath or affirmation, and particularly describing the place to be searched, and the persons or things to be seized.

ARTICLE V

No person shall be held to answer for a capital, or otherwise infamous crime, unless on a presentment or indictment of a grand jury, except in cases arising in the land or naval forces, or in the militia, when in actual service in time of war or public danger; nor shall any person be subject for the same offense to be twice put in jeopardy of life or limb; nor shall be compelled in any criminal case to be a witness against himself, nor be deprived of life, liberty, or property, without due process of law; nor shall private property be taken for public use without just compensation.

ARTICLE VI

In all criminal prosecutions, the accused shall enjoy the right to a speedy and public trial, by an impartial jury of the State and district wherein the crime shall have been committed, which district shall have been previously ascertained by law, and to be informed of the nature and cause of the accusation; to be confronted with the witnesses against him; to have compulsory process for obtaining witnesses in his favor, and to have the assistance of counsel for his defense.

ARTICLE VII

In suits at common law, where the value in controversy shall exceed twenty dollars, the right of trial by jury shall be preserved, and no fact tried by a jury shall be otherwise reexamined in any court of the United States, than according to the rules of the common law.

ARTICLE VIII

Excessive bail shall not be required, nor excessive fines imposed, nor cruel and unusual punishments inflicted.

ARTICLE IX

The enumeration in the Constitution of certain rights shall not be construed to deny or disparage others retained by the people.

ARTICLE X

The powers not delegated to the United States by the Constitution, nor prohibited by it to the States, are reserved to the States respectively, or to the people.

Chapter 9
Jefferson's First Inaugural Address

I realize that this is not a founding document, but it was written by one of the founding fathers (the wisest, in my opinion).

It is included in this book because in this speech Jefferson gives the best description I have ever heard or read of what government *should* be.

"Called upon to undertake the duties of the first executive office of our country, I avail myself of the presence of that portion of my fellow-citizens which is here assembled to express my grateful thanks for the favor with which they have been pleased to look toward me, to declare a sincere consciousness that the task is above my talents, and that I approach it with those anxious and awful presentiments which the greatness of the charge and the weakness of my powers so justify inspire. A rising nation, spread over a wide and fruitful land, traversing all the seas with the rich productions of their industry, engaged in commerce with nations who feel power and forget right, advancing rapidly to destinies beyond the reach of mortal eye--when I contemplate these transcendent objects, and see the honor, the happiness, and the hopes of this beloved country committed to the issue, and the auspices of this day, I shrink from the contemplation and humble myself before the magnitude of the undertaking. Utterly, indeed, should I despair did not the presence of many whom I here see remind me that in the other high authorities provided by our Constitution I shall find resources of wisdom, of virtue, and of zeal on which to rely under all difficulties. To you, then, gentlemen, who are charged with the sovereign funtions of legislation, and to those associated with you, I look with encouragement for that guidance and support which may enable us to steer with safety the vessel in which we are all embarked amidst the conflicting elements of a troubled world.

"During the contest of opinion through which we have passed the animation of discussions and of exertions has sometimes worn an aspect which might impose on strangers unused to think freely and to speak and to write what they think; but this being now decided by the voice of the nation, announced according to the rules of the Constitution, all will of course arrange themselves under the will of the law, and unite in common efforts for the common good. All, too, will bear in mind this sacred principle, that though the will of the majority is in all cases to prevail, that will to be rightful must be reasonable; that the minority possesses their equal rights, which equal law must protect, and to violate would be oppression. Let us, then, fellow-citizens, unite with one heart and one mind. Let us restore to social intercourse that harmony and affection without which liberty and even life itself are but dreary things. And let us reflect that, having banished from our land that religious intolerance under which mankind so long bled and suffered, we have yet gained little if we countenance a political intolerance as despotic, as wicked, and capable of as bitter and bloody persecutions. During the throes and convulsions of the ancient world, during the agonizing spasms of infuriated man, seeking through blood and slaughter his long-lost liberty, it was not wonderful that the agitation of the billows should reach even this distant and peaceful shore; that this should be more felt and feared by some and less by others, and should divide opinions as to measures of safety. But every difference of opinion is not a difference of principle. We have called by different names brethren of the same principle. We are all republicans, we are all federalists. If there be any among us who would wish to dissolve this Union or to change its republican form, let them stand undisturbed as monuments of the safety with which error of opinion may be tolerated where reason is left free to combat it. I know, indeed, that some honest men fear that a republican government can not be strong, that this Government is not strong enough; but would the honest patriot, in the full tide of successful experiment, abandon a government which has so far kept us free and firm on the theoretic and visionary fear that this Government, the world's best hope, may by possibility want energy to preserve itself? I trust not. I believe this, on the contrary, the strongest Government on earth. I believe it the only one where every man, at the call of the law, would fly to the standard of the law, and would meet invasions of the public order as his own personal concern. Sometimes it is said that man can not be trusted with the government of himself. Can he, then, be trusted with the government of others? Or have we found angels in the forms of kings to govern him? Let history answer this question.

"Let us, then, with courage and confidence pursue our own Federal and Republican principles, our attachment to union and representative government. Kindly separated by nature and a wide ocean from the exterminating havoc of one quarter of the globe; too high-minded to endure the degradations of the others; possessing a chosen country, with room enough for our decendants to the thousandth and thousandth generation; entertaining a due sense of our equal right to the use of our own faculties, to the acquisitions of our own industry, to honor and confidence from our fellow-citizens, resulting not from birth, but from our actions and their sense of them; enlightened by a benign religion, professed, indeed, and practiced in various forms, yet all of them inculcating honesty, truth, temperance, gratitude, and the love of man; acknowledging and adoring an overruling Providence, which by all its dispensations proves that it delights in the happiness of man here and his greater happiness hereafter--with all these blessings, what more is necessary to make us a happy and a prosperous people? Still one thing more, fellow-citizens-- a wise and frugal Government, which shall restrain men from injuring one another, shall leave them otherwise free to regulate their own pursuits of industry and improvement, and shall not take from the mouth of labor the bread it has earned. This is the sum of good government, and this is necessary to close the circle of our felicities.

"About to enter, fellow-citizens, on the exercise of duties which comprehend everything dear and valuable to you, it is proper you should understand what I deem the essential principles of our Government, and consequently those which ought to shape its Administration. I will compress them within the narrowest compass they will bear, stating the general principle, but not all its limitations. Equal and exact justice to all men, of whatever state or persuasion, religious or political; peace, commerce, and honest friendship with all nations, entangling alliances with none; the support of the State governments in all their rights, as the most competent administrations for our domestic concerns and the surest bulwarks against antirepublican tendencies; the preservation of the General Government in its whole constitutional vigor, as the sheet anchor of our peace at home and safety abroad; a jealous care of the right of election by the people--a mild and safe corrective of abuses which are lopped by the sword of revolution where peaceable remedies are unprovided; absolute acquiescence in the decisions of the majority, the vital principle and immediate parent of despotism; a well-disciplined militia, our best reliance in peace and for the first moments of war, till regulars may relieve them; the supremacy of the civil over the military authority; economy in the public expense, that labor may be lightly burthened; the honest payment of our debts and sacred preservation of the public faith; encouragement of agriculture, and of commerce as its handmaid; the diffusion of information and arraignment of all abuses at the bar of the public reason; freedom of religion; freedom of the press, and freedom of person under the protection of the habeas corpus, and trial by juries impartially selected. These principles form the bright constellation which has gone before us and guided our steps through an age of revolution and reformation. The wisdom of our sages and blood of our heroes have been devoted to their attainment. They should be the creed of our political faith, the text of civic instruction, the touchstone by which to try the services of those we trust; and should we wander from them in moments of error or of alarm, let us hasten to retrace our steps and to regain the road which alone leads to peace, liberty, and safety.

"I repair, then, fellow-citizens, to the post you have assigned me. With experience enough in subordinate offices to have seen the difficulties of this the greatest of all, I have learnt to expect that it will rarely fall to the lot of imperfect men to retire from this station with the reputation and the favor which bring him into it. Without pretentions to that high confidence you respond in our first and greatest revolutionary character, whose preeminent service has entitled him to the first place in his country's love and destined for him the fairest page in the volume of faithful history, I ask so much confidence only as may give firmness and effect to the legal administration of your affairs. I shall often go wrong through defect of judgment. When right, I shall often be thought wrong by those whose positions will not command a view of the whole ground. I ask your indulgence for my own errors, which will never be intentional, and your support against the errors of others, who may condemn what they would not if seen in all its parts. The approbation implied by your suffrage is a great consolation to me for the past, and my future solicitude will be to retain the good opinion of those who have bestowed it in advance, to conciliate that of others by doing them all the good in my power, and to be instrumental to the hapiness and freedom of all.

"Relying, then, on the patronage of your good will, I advance with obedience to the work, ready to retire from it whenever you become sensible how much better choice it is in your power to make. And may that Infinite Power which rules the destinies of the universe lead our councils to what is best, and give them a favorable issue for your peace and prosperity.[97]

Chapter 10
Additional Amendments

The good and the bad.

ARTICLE XI
Passed by Congress March 5, 1794 – Ratified January 8, 1798

The judicial power of the United States shall not be construed to extend to any suit in law or equity commenced or prosecuted against one of the United States by citizens of another State, or by citizens or subjects of any foreign State.

ARTICLE XII
Passed by Congress December 12, 1803 – Ratified September 25, 1804

The electors shall meet in their respective States, and vote by ballot for President and Vice President, one of whom, at least, shall not be an inhabitant of the same State with themselves; they shall name in their ballots the person voted for as President, and in distinct ballots, the person voted for as Vice President, and they shall make distinct lists of all persons voted for as President and of all persons voted for as Vice President, and of the number of votes for each, which lists they shall sign and certify, and transmit sealed to the seat of the government of the United States, directed to the President of the Senate; --The President of the Senate shall, in the presence of the Senate and House of Representatives, open all the certificates and the votes shall then be counted;--The person having the greatest number of votes for President, shall be the President, if such number be a majority of the whole number of electors appointed; and if no person have such majority, then from the persons having the highest numbers not exceeding three on the list of those voted for as President, the House of Representatives shall choose immediately, by ballot, the President. But in choosing the President, the votes shall be taken by States, the representation from each State having one vote; a quorum for this purpose shall consist of a member or members from two-thirds of the States, and a majority of all the States shall be necessary to a choice. And if the House of Representatives shall not choose a President whenever the right of choice shall devolve upon them, before the fourth day of

March next following, then the Vice President shall act as President, as is in the case of the death or other constitutional disability of the President. The person having the greatest number of votes as Vice President shall be the Vice President, if such number be a majority of the whole number of electors appointed, and if no person have a majority then from the two highest numbers on the list, the Senate shall choose the Vice President; a quorum for the purpose shall consist of two thirds of the whole number of Senators, and a majority of the whole number shall be necessary to a choice. But no person constitutionally ineligible to the office of President shall be eligible to that of Vice President of the United States.

ARTICLE XIII
Passed by Congress February 1, 1865 – Ratified December 18, 1866

Section 1. Neither slavery nor involuntary servitude, except as punishment for a crime whereof the party shall have been duly convicted, shall exist within the United States, or any place subject to their jurisdiction.

Section 2. Congress shall have power to enforce this article by appropriate legislation.

ARTICLE XIV
Passed by Congress June 16, 1866 – Ratified July 28, 1868

Section 1. All persons born or naturalized in the United States, and subject to the jurisdiction thereof, are citizens of the United States and of the State wherein they reside. No State shall make or enforce any law which shall abridge the privileges or immunities of citizens of the United States; nor shall any State deprive any person of life, liberty, or property, without due process of law; nor deny to any person within its jurisdiction the equal protection of the laws.

Section 2. Representatives shall be apportioned among the several States according to their respective numbers, counting the whole number of persons in each State, excluding Indians not taxed. But when the right to vote at any election for the choice of electors for President and Vice President of the United States, representatives in Congress, the executive and judicial officers of a State, or the members of the legislature thereof, is denied to any of the male inhabitants of such State, being twenty-one years of age, and citizens of the United States, or in any way abridged, except for participation in rebellion, or other crime, the basis of representation therein shall be reduced in the proportion which the number of such male citizens shall bear to the whole number of male citizens twenty-one years of age in such State.

Section 3. No person shall be a senator or representative in Congress, or elector of President and Vice President, or hold any office, civil or military, under the United States, or under any State, who having previously taken an oath, as a member of Congress, or as an officer of the United States, or a member of any State legislature, or as an executive or judicial officer of any State, to support the Constitution of the United States, shall have engaged in insurrection or rebellion against the same, or given aid or comfort to the enemies thereof. But Congress may by a vote of two-thirds of each House, remove such disability.

Section 4. The validity of the public debt of the United States, authorized by law, including debts incurred for payment of pensions and bounties for services in suppressing insurrection or rebellion, shall not be questioned. But neither the United States nor any State shall assume or pay any debt or obligation incurred in aid of insurrection or rebellion against the United States, or any claim for the loss or emancipation of any slave; but all such debts, obligations, and claims shall be held illegal and void.

Section 5. The Congress shall have power to enforce, by appropriate legislation, the provisions of this article.

ADDITIONAL AMENDMENTS

~*~

"All persons *born or naturalized* in the United States, and subject to the jurisdiction thereof, are citizens of the United States and of the State wherein they reside." This *does not* apply to *anybody* who crosses the border *illegally*.

ARTICLE XV
Passed by Congress February 26, 1869 – Ratified March 30, 1870

Section 1. The right of citizens of the United States to vote shall not be denied or abridged by the United States or by any State on account of race, color, or previous condition of servitude.

Section 2. The Congress shall have power to enforce this article by appropriate legislation.

ARTICLE XVI
Passed by Congress July 12, 1909 – Ratified February 25, 1913

The Congress shall have power to lay and collect taxes on incomes, from whatever source derived, without apportionment among the several States, and without regard to any census or enumeration.

~*~

So much for not taking from the mouth of labor the bread it has earned.

ARTICLE XVII
Passed by Congress May 16, 1912 – Ratified May 31, 1913

Section 1. The Senate of the United States shall be composed of two senators from each State, elected by the people thereof, for six years; and each senator shall have one vote. The electors in each State shall have the qualifications requisite for electors of the most numerous branch of the State legislature.

Section 2. When vacancies happen in the representation of any State in the Senate, the executive authority of such State shall issue writs of election to fill such vacancies: *Provided,* That the legislature of any State may empower the executive thereof to make temporary appointments until the people fill the vacancies by election as the legislature may direct.

Section 3. This amendment shall not be so construed as to affect the election or term of any senator chosen before it becomes valid as part of the Constitution.

ADDITIONAL AMENDMENTS

ARTICLE XVIII
Passed by Congress December 18, 1917 – Ratified January 29, 1919

Section 1. After one year from the ratification of this article, the manufacture, sale, or transportation of intoxicating liquors within, the importation thereof into, or the exportation thereof from the United States and all territory subject to the jurisdiction thereof for beverage purposes is hereby prohibited.

Section 2. The Congress and the several States shall have concurrent power to enforce this article by appropriate legislation.

Section 3. This article shall be inoperative unless it shall have been ratified as an amendment to the Constitution by the legislatures of the several States, as provided in the Constitution, within seven years from the date of the submission hereof to the States by Congress.

ARTICLE XIX
Passed by Congress June 5, 1919 – Ratified August 26, 1920

Section 1. The right of citizens of the United States to vote shall not be denied or abridged by the United States or by any State on account of sex.

Section 2. The Congress shall have power by appropriate legislation to enforce the provisions of this article.

ARTICLE XX
Passed by Congress March 3, 1932 – Ratified February 6, 1933

Section 1. The terms of the President and Vice President shall end at noon on the 20th day of January, and the terms of Senators and Representatives at noon on the 3d day of January, of the years in which such terms would have ended if this article had not been ratified; and the terms of their successors shall then begin.

Section 2. The Congress shall assemble at least once in every year, and such meeting shall begin at noon on the 3d day of January, unless they shall appoint a different day.

Section 3. If, at the time fixed for the beginning of the term of the President, the President-elect shall have died, the Vice President-elect shall become President. If a President shall not have been chosen before the time fixed for the beginning of his term, or if the President-elect shall have failed to qualify, then the Vice President-elect shall act as President until a President shall have qualified; and the Congress may by law provide for the case wherein neither a President-elect nor a Vice President-elect shall have qualified, declaring who shall then act as President, or the manner in which one who is to act shall be selected, and such person shall act accordingly until a President or Vice President shall have qualified.

Section 4. The Congress may by law provide for the case of the death of any of the persons from whom the House of Representatives may choose a President whenever the right of choice shall have devolved upon them, and for the case of the death of any of the persons from whom the Senate may choose a Vice President whenever the right of choice shall have devolved upon them.

Section 5. Sections 1 and 2 shall take effect on the 15th day of October following the ratification of this article.

Section 6. This article shall be inoperative unless it shall have been ratified as an amendment to the Constitution by the legislatures of three-fourths of the several States within seven years from the date of its submission.

ARTICLE XXI
Passed by Congress February 20, 1933 – Ratified December 5, 1933

Section 1. The eighteenth article of amendment to the Constitution of the United States is hereby repealed.

Section 2. The transportation or importation into any State, Territory, or possession of the United States for delivery or use therein of intoxicating liquors in violation of the laws thereof, is hereby prohibited.

Section 3. This article shall be inoperative unless it shall have been ratified as an amendment to the Constitution by conventions in the several States, as provided in the Constitution, within seven years from the date of the submission thereof to the States by the Congress.

ARTICLE XXII
Passed by Congress March 12, 1947 – Ratified February 26, 1951

Section 1. No person shall be elected to the office of the President more than twice, and no person who has held the office of President, or acted as President, for more than two years of a term to which some other person was elected President shall be elected to the office of the President more than once.

But this article shall not apply to any person holding the office of President when this article was proposed by Congress, and shall not prevent any person who may be holding the office of President, or acting as President during the term within which this article becomes operative from holding the office of President or acting as President during the remainder of such term.

Section 2. This article shall be inoperative unless it shall have been ratified as an amendment to the Constitution by the legislatures of three fourths of the several States within seven years from the date of its submission to the States by the Congress.

ARTICLE XXIII
Passed by Congress June 16, 1960 – Ratified March 29, 1961

Section 1. The District constituting the seat of Government of the United States shall appoint in such manner as the Congress may direct:

A number of electors of President and Vice President equal to the whole number of Senators and Representatives in Congress to which the District would be entitled if it were a State, but in no event more than the least populous state; they shall be in addition to those appointed by the states, but shall be considered, for the purpose of the election of President and Vice President, to be electors appointed by a State; and they shall meet in the District and perform such duties as provided by the twelfth article of amendment.

Section 2. The Congress shall have power to enforce this article by appropriate legislation.

ARTICLE XXIV
Passed by Congress August 27, 1962 – Ratified January 23, 1964

Section 1. The right of citizens of the United

States to vote in any primary or other election for President or Vice President, for electors for President or Vice President, or for Senator or Representative in Congress, shall not be denied or abridged by the United States or any State by reason of failure to pay any poll tax or other tax.

Section 2. The Congress shall have the power to enforce this article by appropriate legislation.

ARTICLE XXV
Passed by Congress July 6, 1965 – Ratified February 10, 1967

Section 1. In case of the removal of the President from office or his death or resignation, the Vice President shall be come President.

Section 2. Whenever there is a vacancy in the office of the Vice President, the President shall nominate a Vice President who shall take the office upon confirmation by a majority vote of both houses of Congress.

Section 3. Whenever the President transmits to the President pro tempore of the Senate and the Speaker of the House of Representatives his written declaration that he is unable to discharge the powers and duties of his office, and until he transmits to them a written declaration to the contrary, such powers and duties shall be discharged by the Vice President as Acting

President.

Section 4. Whenever the Vice President and a majority of either the principal officers of the executive departments or of such other body as Congress may by law provide, transmit to the President pro tempore of the Senate and the Speaker of the House of Representatives their written declaration that the President is unable to discharge the powers and duties of his office, the Vice President shall immediately assume the powers and duties of the office as Acting President.

Thereafter, when the President transmits to the President pro tempore of the Senate and the Speaker of the House of Representatives his written declaration that no inability exists, he shall resume the powers and duties of his office unless the Vice President and a majority of either the principal officers of the executive department or of such other body as Congress may by law provide, transmit within four days to the President pro tempore of the Senate and the Speaker of the House of Representatives their written declaration that the President is unable to discharge the powers and duties of his office. Thereupon Congress shall decide the issue, assembling within 48 hours if not in session. If the Congress, within 21 days after receipt of the latter written declaration, or, if Congress is not in session, within 21 days after

Chapter 11
A Necessary Evil

"Society in every state is a blessing, but Government, even in its best state, is but a necessary evil; in its worst state, an intolerable one." - Thomas Paine[102]

And let's not forget what Benjamin Franklin said:
"They who can give up essential Liberty to obtain a little temporary Safety deserve neither Liberty nor Safety."[103]

COVID-19 restrictions anyone?

Avoiding Tyranny
Jonathan Mayhew, a minister who lectured at

Harvard in 1766 had this to say about colonists feelings on the Stamp Act:

"The king is as much bound by his oath not to infringe the legal rights of the people, as the people are bound to yield subjection to him. From whence it follows that as soon as the prince sets himself above the law, he loses the king in the tyrant. He does, to all intents and purposes, unking himself."[104]

From a letter that Thomas Jefferson wrote to a friend on September 20, 1810:

"A strict observance of the written laws is doubtless *one* of the high duties of a good citizen, but it is not *the highest*. The laws of necessity, of self-preservation, of saving our country when in danger, are of higher obligation. To lose our country by a scrupulous adherence to written law, would be to lose the law itself, with life, liberty, property and all those who are enjoying them with us; thus absurdly sacrificing the end to the means."[105]

From Thomas Jefferson's January 30, 1787 letter to James Madison:

"I hold it that a little rebellion now and then is a good thing, & as necessary in the political world as storms in the physical. Unsuccessful rebellions indeed generally establish the encroachments on the rights of the people which have produced them. An observation of this truth should render honest republican governors so mild in their punishment of rebellions, as not to discourage them too much. It is a medicine necessary for the sound health of government...."[106]

Good Government Explained

Good government sounds like a paradox, but it is possible if the government is small and not invasive. Our government started out that way, but unfortunetly it has grown beyond what it was supposed to be.

~*~

From a letter that Thomas Jefferson wrote to Major John Cartwright (an Englishman who supported America's revolt)[107] on June 5, 1824:

"With respect to our State and federal governments, I do not think their relations correctly understood by foreigners. They generally suppose the former subordinate to the latter. But this is not the case. They are coordinate departments of one simple and integral whole. To the State governments are reserved all legislation and administration, in affairs which concern their own citizens only, and to the federal government is given whatever concerns foreigners, or the citizens of other States; these functions alone being made federal. The one is the domestic, the other the foreign branch of the same government; neither having control over the other, but within its own department. There are one or two exceptions only to this partition of power."[108]

From Thomas Jefferson's January 26, 1799 letter to Elbridge Gerry (then diplomat to France):

"I am for preserving to the States the powers not yielded by them to the Union, & to the legislature of the Union it's constitutional share in the division of powers; and I am not for transferring all the powers of the States to the general government, & all those of that government to the Executive branch. I am for a government rigorously frugal & simple, applying all the possible savings of the public revenue to the discharge of the national debt; and not for a multiplication of officers & salaries merely to make partisans, & for increasing by every device, the public debt, on the principle of it's being a public blessing. I am for relying, for internal defence, on our militia solely, till actual invasion, and for such a naval force only as may protect our coasts and harbors from such depredations as we have experienced; and not for a standing army in time of peace, which may overawe the public sentiment; nor for a navy, which, by it's own expenses and the eternal wars in which it will implicate us, will grind us with public burthens, & sink us under them. I am for free commerce with all nations; political connection with none; & little or no diplomatic establishment. And I am not for linking ourselves by new treaties with the quarrels of Europe; entering that field of slaughter to preserve their balance, or joining in the confederacy of kings to war against the principles of liberty. I am for freedom of religion, & against all maneuvers to bring about a legal ascendancy of one sect over another: for freedom of the press, & against all violations of the constitution to silence by force & not by reason the complaints or criticisms, just or unjust, of our citizens against the conduct of their agents."[109]

~*~

From Thomas Jefferson's December 20, 1787 letter to James Madison:

"I think our governments will remain virtuous for many centuries; as long as they are chiefly agricultural; and this will be as long as there shall be vacant lands in any part of America. When they get piled upon one another in large cities, as in Europe, they will become corrupt as in Europe.

Above all things I hope the education of the common people will be attended to; convinced that on their good sense we may rely with the most security for the preservation of a due degree of liberty...."[110]

Voting for Politicians

Here we have a description of a typical politician:

"He who permits himself to tell a lie once, finds it much easier to do it a second and third time, till at length it becomes habitual; he tells lies without attending to it, and truths without the world's believing him. This falsehood of the tongue leads to that of the heart, and in time depraves all its good dispositions." - Thomas Jefferson[111]

I don't think Jefferson was specifically talking about politicians, just humans in general. But this does seem to be a more prevalent trait in politicians...

~*~

"Let each citizen remember at the moment he is offering his vote that he is not making a present or a compliment to please an individual—or at least that he ought not so to do; but that he is executing one of the most solemn trusts in human society for which he is accountable to God and his country." - Samuel Adams in 1781.[112]

And here Noah Webster gives us a good rule of thumb for voting:

"In selecting men for office, let principle be your guide. Regard not the particular sect [party] of the candidate—look to his character....It is alleged by men of loose principles or defective views of the subject that religion and morality are not necessary or important Scriptures teach a different doctrine. They direct that rulers should be men "who rule in the fear of God, able men, such as fear God, men of truth, hating covetousness".[113]

He also gives us a blast from the future:

"God commands you to choose for rulers, just men who will rule in the fear of God. The preservation of a republican government depends on the faithful discharge of this duty; if the citizens neglect their duty and place unprincipled men in office, the government will soon be corrupted; laws will be made, not for the public good, so much as for selfish or local purposes; corrupt or incompetent men will be appointed to execute the laws; the public revenues will be squandered on unworthy men; and the rights of the citizens will be violated or disreguarded."[114]

Chapter 12
Freedom of the Press

"Whereas it appeareth that however certain forms of government are better calculated than others to protect individuals in the free exercise of their natural rights, and are at the same time themselves better guarded against degeneracy, yet experience hath shown, that even under the best forms, those entrusted with power have, in time, and by slow operrations, perverted it into tyranny; and it is believed that the most effectual means of preventing this would be, to illuminate, as far as practicable, the minds of the people at large, and more especially to give them knowledge of those facts, with history exhibiteth, that, possessed thereby of the experiences of other ages and countries, they may be enabled to know ambition under all its shapes, and prompt to exert their natural powers to defeat its purposes." - from

Thomas Jefferson's 1778 'A Bill for the More General Diffusion of Knowledge'.[115]

"I am persuaded myself that the good sense of the people will always be found to be the best army. They may be led astray for a moment, but will soon correct themselves. The people are the only censors of their governors: and even their errors will tend to keep these to the true principles of their institution. To punish these errors too severely would be to suppress the only safeguard of the public liberty. The way to prevent these irregular interpositions of the people is to give them full information of their affairs thro' the channel of the public papers, & to contrive that those papers should penetrate the whole mass of the people. The basis of our governments being the opinion of the people, the very first object should be to keep that right; and were it left to me to decide whether we should have a government without newspapers or newspapers without a government, I should not hesitate a moment to prefer the latter. But I should mean that every man should recieve those papers & be capable of reading them. I am convinced that those societies (as the Indians) which live without government enjoy in their general mass an infinitely greater degree of happiness than those who live under the European governments. Among the former, public opinion is in the place of law, & restrains morals as powerfully as laws ever did anywhere. Among the latter, under pretence of governing they have divided their nations into two classes, wolves & sheep. I do not exaggerate. This is a true picture of Europe. Cherish therefore the spirit of our people, and keep alive their attention. Do not be too severe upon their errors, but reclaim them by enlightening them. If once they become inattentive to the public affairs, you & I, & Congress & Assemblies, judges & governors shall all become wolves." - from Thomas Jefferson's January 16, 1787 letter to Edward Carrington (Lieutenant Colonel in the Continental Army) reguarding Shays' Rebellion.[116]

"No experiment can be more interesting than that we are now trying, and which we trust will end in establishing the fact, that man may be governed by reason and truth. Our first object should therefore be, to leave open to him all the avenues to truth. The most effectual hitherto found, is the freedom of the press. It is therefore, the first shut up by those who fear the investigation of their actions. The firmness with which the people have withstood the late abuses of the press, the discernment they have manifested between truth and falsehood, show that they may safely be trusted to hear everything true and false, and to form correct judgement between them. As little is it necessary to impose on their senses, or dazzle their minds by pomp, splendor, or forms. Instead of this artificial, how much surer is that real respect, which results from the use of their reason, and habit of bringing everything to the test of common sense.

"I hold it, therefore, certain, that to open the doors of truth, and to fortify the habit of testing everything by reason, are the most effectual manacles we can rivet on the hands of our successors to prevent their manacling the people with their own consent. The panic into which they were artfully thrown in 1798, the frenzy which was excited in them by their enemies against their apparent readiness to abandon all the principles established for their own protection, seemed for awhile to countenance the opinions of those who say they cannot be trusted with their own government. But I never doubted their rallying; and they did rally much sooner than I expected. On the whole, that experiment on their credulity has confirmed my confidence in their ultimate good sense and virtue...." - from Thomas Jefferson's June 28, 1804 letter to John Tyler Sr (father of America's tenth President).[117]

"If a nation expects to be ignorant and free, in a

state of civilization, it expects what never was and never will be. The functionaries of every government have propensities to command at will the liberty and property of their constituents. There is no safe deposit for these but with the people themselves; nor can they be safe with them without information. Where the press is free, and every man able to read, all is safe." - from Thomas Jefferson's January 6, 1816 letter to a friend.[118]

Chapter 13
Never Forget

"The tree of liberty must be refreshed from time to time with the blood of patriots & tyrants." - from Thomas Jefferson's November 13, 1787 letter to William S. Smith (husband of John Adams' daughter Abigail "Nabby").[119]

~*~

Even the definition of patriotism has been changed. This is what it says on Merriam-Webster.com:

"Love for or devotion to one's country."[120]

Now contrast that with this definition in Noah Webster's 1828 Dictionary:

"Love of one's country; the passion which aims to serve one's country, either in defending it from invasion, or protecting its rights and maintaining its laws and institutions in vigor and purity. Patriotism is the characteristic of a good citizen, the noblest passion that animates a man in the character of a citizen."[121]

~*~

"The fundamental source of all your errors, sophisms, and false reasonings, is a total ignorance of the rights of mankind. Were you once to become aquainted with these, you could never entertain a thought that all men are not, by nature, entitled to a parity of privileges. You would be convinced that natural liberty is a gift of the beneficent Creator to the whole human race; and that civil liberty is founded in that and cannot be wrested from any people, without the most manifest violation of justice." - from a pamphlet that Alexander Hamilton wrote in 1775.[122]

"The liberties of our country, the freedom of our civil Constitution, are worth defending at all hazards; and it is our duty to defend them against all attacks. We have received them as a fair inheritance from our worthy ancestors: they purchased them for us with toil and danger and expense of treasure and blood, and transmitted them to us with care and diligence. It will bring an everlasting mark of infamy on the present generation, enlighten as it is, if we should suffer them to be wrested from us by violence without a struggle or to be cheated out of them by the artifices of false and designing men." - Samuel Adams[123]

"Posterity! You will never know, how much it cost the present Generation, to preserve your Freedom! I hope you will make a good Use of it. If you do not, I shall repent in Heaven, that I ever took half the Pains to preserve it." - John Adams on April 26, 1777[124]

Never forget the sacrifices that were made by those early Americans. It doesn't matter if your family has been here since the *Mayflower*, or if your family didn't come until the early 20th century, or if you yourself are an immigrant. You owe these people a debt of gratitude. And the best way to pay them back is to stand up for your rights as an American. Otherwise they fought for nothing.

Chapter 14
In God We Trust

First, the word of God, Who cannot and should not be argued with:

"If my people who are called by my name humble themselves, and pray and seek my face and turn from their wicked ways, then I will hear from heaven and will forgive their sin and heal their land." - 2 Chronicles 7:14

And now the words of some of the wise men who understood that:

Death is more eligible than slavery. A free-born people are not required by the religion of Jesus Christ to submit to tyranny, but may make use of such power as God has given them to recover and support their laws and liberties....[We] implore the Ruler above the skies, that He would make bare His arm in defense of His Church and people, and let

Israel go. - The men of Marlborough, Massachusetts in early 1773.[125]

Resistance to tyranny becomes the Christian and social duty of each individual....Continue steadfast, and with a proper sense of your dependence on God, nobly defend those rights which heaven gave, and no man ought to take from us. - Massachusetts Provincial Congress in 1774.[126]

"Statesmen...may plan and speculate for liberty, but it is religion and morality alone which can establish the principles upon which freedom can securely stand.
"The only foundation of a free constitution is pure virtue, and if this cannot be inspired into our people in a greater measure, than they have it now, they may change their rulers and the forms of government, but they will not obtain a lasting liberty." - John Adams on June 21, 1776.[127]

"A general dissolution of principles and manners will more surely overthrow the liberties of America than the whole force of the common enemy. While the people are virtuous they cannot be subdued; but when once they lose their virtue, they will be ready to surrender their liberties to the first external or internal invader. How necessary then is it for those who are determined to transmit the blessings of liberty as a fair inheritance to posterity, to associate on public principles in support of public virtue." - Samuel Adams in a 1779 letter to James Warren.[128]

"Of all the dispositions and habits which lead to political prosperity, religion and morality are indespensable supports. In vain would that man claim the tribute of patriotism who should labor to subvert these great pillars of human happiness— these firmest props of the duties of men and citizens. The mere politician, equally with the pious man, ought to respect and to cherish them. A volume could not trace all their connections with private and public felicity. Let it simply be asked, Where is the security for property, for repuation, for life, if the sense of religious obligation, desert the oaths which are the instruments of investigation in courts of justice?" And let us with caution indulge the supposition that morality can be maintained without religion. Whatever may be conceded to the influence of refiened education on minds of peculiar structure, reason and experience both forbid us to expect that national morality can prevail in exclusion of religious principle.

"It is substantially true that virtue or morality is a necessary spring of popular government. The rule indeed extends with more or less force to every species of free government. Who that is a sincere friend to it can look with indifference upon attempts to shake the foundation of the fabric?" - from George Washington's Farewell Address in 1796.[129]

"We have no government armed with power capable of contending with human passions unbridled by morality and religion. Avarice, ambition, revenge, or gallantry would break the strongest cords of our Constitution as a whale goes through a net. Our Constitution was made only for a moral and religious people. It is wholly inadequate to the government of any other." - 1798 letter from John Adams to the Militia of Massachusetts.[130]

"Our dangers are of two kinds, those which affect our religion, and those which affect our government. They are, however, so closely allied that they cannot, with propriety, be separated. The foundations which support the interest of Christianity, are also necessary to support a free and equal government like our own....
"To the kindly influence of Christianity we owe that degree of civil freedom, and political and social happiness which mankind now enjoys. In

proportion as the genuine effects of Christianity are diminished in any nation, either through unbelief or the corruption of its doctrine, or the neglect of its institutions; in the same proportion will the people of that nation recede from the blessings of genuine freedom, and approximate the miseries of complete despotism. I hold this to be a truth confirmed by experience. If so, it follows, that all efforts made to destroy the foundations of our holy religion, ultimately tend to the subversion also of our political freedom and happiness. Whenever the pillars of Christianity shall be overthrown, our present republican forms of government, and all the blessings which flow from them, must fall with them." - from one of Jedidiah Morse's 1799 sermons to the First Church of Charlestown, Massachusetts, 'If the foundations be destroyed, what can the righteous do?'.[131] (Besides being a minister, Jedidiah also wrote the first American Geography textbook, and he was the father of inventor Samuel Morse.)[132]

"No nation has ever yet existed or been governed without religion—nor can be. The Christian religion is the best religion that has been given to man and I, as Chief Magistrate of this nation, am bound to give it the sanction of my example." - Thomas Jefferson to a friend while walking to church at some point during his time as President.[133]

"I shall need, too, the favor of that Being in Whose hands we are, Who led our fathers, as Israel of old, from their native land and planted them in a country flowing with all the necessaries and comforts of life; Who has covered our infancy with His providence and our riper years with His wisdom and power, and to Whose goodness I ask you to join in suplications with me that He will so enlighten the minds of your servants, guide their councils, and prosper their measures that whatsoever they do shall result in your good and shall secure to you the peace, friendship, and approbation of all nations." - from Thomas Jefferson's Second Inaugural Address.[134]

"The general Principles, on which the Fathers Achieved Independence, were the only Principles in which, that beautiful Assembly of young Gentlemen could Unite, and these Principles only could be intended by them in their Address, or by me in my Answer. And what were these general Principles? I answer, the general Principles of Christianity, in which all those Sects were United: And the general Principles of English and American

Liberty, in which all those young Men United, and which had United all Parties in America, in Majorities Sufficient to assert and maintain her Independence.

Now I will avow, that I then believed, and now believe, that those general Principles of Christianity, are as eternal and immutable, as the Existence and Attributes of God: and that those Principles of Liberty, are as unalterable as human Nature and our terrestrial, mundane System." - John Adams in a letter to Thomas Jefferson, dated June 28, 1813.[135]

"I have always considered Christianity as the strong ground of republicanism. The spirit is opposed, not only to the splendor, but even to the very forms of monarchy, and many of its precepts have for their objects republican liberty and equality as well as simplicity, integrity, and economy in government. It is only necessary for republicanism to ally itself to the Christian religion to overturn all the corrupted political and religious institutions in the world." - Dr. Benjamin Rush in a letter to Thomas Jefferson, dated August 22, 1800.[136]

"Without morals a republic cannot subsist any

length of time; therefore who are decrying the Christian religion, whose morality is so sublime and pure...are undermining the solid foundation of morals, the best security for the duration of free governments." - Charles Carroll (Signer of the Declaration from Maryland.)[137]

"An attempt to conduct the affairs of a free government with wisdom and impartiality, and to preserve the just rights of all classes of citizens, without the guidance of Divine precepts, will certainly end in disappointment. God is the supreme moral Governor of the world He has made, and as He Himself governs with perfect rectitude, He requires His rational creatures to govern themselves in like manner. If men will not submit to be controlled by His laws, He will punish them by the evils resulting from their own disobedience....

"Any system of education, therefore, which limits instruction to the arts and sciences and rejects the aids of religion in forming the characters of citizens, is essentially defective....

"In my view, the Christian religion is the most important and one of the first things in which all children, under a free government ought to be instructed....No truth is more evident to my mind than that the Christian religion must be the basis of any government intended to secure the rights and privileges of a free people." - Noah Webster[138]

"We have staked the whole future of the American civilization, not upon the power of government, far from it. We have staked the future...upon the capacity of each and all of us to govern ourselves, to control ourselves, to sustain ourselves, according to the Ten Commandments of God." - James Madison [139]

This is the reason that our country is falling apart. Instead of keeping to our morals we have become a secular nation.

If we are to have any hope of getting our country back the way it used to be, the way it was meant to be, then we must turn back to God.

And now I will leave you with the words of two of our Presidents, Andrew Jackson and Abraham Lincoln. Until this point I have been trying to stick to quotes from our colonial leaders only, but I couldn't think of a better way to end this book than with these reminders.

From Andrew Jackson's 1837 Farewell Address:

"But you must remember, my fellow citizens,

that eternal vigilance by the people is the price of liberty, and that you must pay the price if you wish to secure the blessing.

"You have no longer any cause to fear danger from abroad; your strength and power are well known throughout the civilized world, as well as the high and gallant bearing of your sons. It is from within, among yourselves—from cupidity, from corruption, from disappointed ambition and inordinate thirst for power—that factions will be formed and liberty endangered. It is against such designs, whatever disguise the actors may assume, that you have especially to guard yourselves. You have the highest of human trusts committed to your care. Providence has showered on this favored land blessings without number, and has chosen you as the guardians of freedom, to preserve it for the benefit of the human race. May He who holds in His hands the destinies of nations make you worthy of the favors He has bestowed and enable you, with pure hearts and pure hands and sleepless vigilance, to guard and defend to the end of time the great charge He has committed to your keeping."[140]

And from Abraham Lincoln's Gettysburg Address on November 19, 1863:

"It is for us, the living, rather, to be dedicated here to the unfinished work which they who fought here have thus far so nobly advanced. It is rather for us to be here dedicated to the great task remaining before us—that from these honored dead we take increased devotion to that cause for which they gave the last full measure of devotion; that we here highly resolve that these dead shall not have died in vain; that this nation, under God, shall have a new birth of freedom; and that government of the people, by the people, for the people, shall not perish from the earth."

God bless America.

ACKNOWLEDGEMENTS

I want to thank Anna for suggesting that I write a history book.

And I woud also like to thank my editor, Rhea, for all her valuable input.

About the Author

Rebecca Bastian was homeschooled by her parents, who taught her to love God and Country, in that order. And she continues to educate herself by reading books and articles about things that interest her, such as history (but especially American history).

You can visit her website at:
www.rebeccajbastian.wordpress.com

INDEX

Adams, Abigail, 41
Adams, John, 7, 11, 14, 33, 41 126, 128, 130, 132, 135
Adams, Samuel, 120, 128, 131
Administration of Justice Act, 15
America, 1, 2, 3, 4, 5, 6, 9, 11, 17, 23, 39, 41, 45, 46, 47, 52, 57, 59, 69, 116, 118, 124, 130, 135, 139
American Revolution, 18, 31, 43, 56
Army, British, 26, 27, 30, 52
Army, U.S., 72
Arnold, Benedict, 31, 53
Articles of Confederation, 78
Atlantic Ocean, 29
Babel, 58, 81
Barbados, 29
Bartlett, Josiah, 47
Bartlett, Mary, 47
Beaver, 12
Billings, William, 29
Bill of Rights, 84
Birch, Samuel, 43
Boleyn, Anne, 2
Boston, Massachusetts, 8, 10, 12, 13, 15, 19, 29, 43, 47
Boston Harbor, 12

INDEX

Boston Massacre, 10, 11
Boston Port Act, 15, 23
Boston Tea Party, 12, 14
Britain, 5, 7, 9, 16, 30, 45, 46, 47
British West Indies, 29
Brooklyn, New York, 26, 28
Brown University, 30
Burgoyne, John, 29, 44
Carrington, Edward, 123
Carroll, Charles, 136
Cartwright, John, 116
Catholic, 2
Charles II (king), 3
Charlestown, Massachusetts, 133
Chase, Samuel, 40
Christian, 4, 130, 133, 135, 136
Christianity, 3, 132, 133, 134, 135
Church of England, 1, 2
Clinton, Henry, 29
Colonel Chester, 28
Common Sense, 44
Concord, Massachusetts, 18, 19
Congress, 59, 60, 62, 63, 64, 65, 67, 68, 69, 70, 71, 72, 73, 74, 75, 76, 77, 78, 84, 98, 100, 101, 102, 103, 104, 105, 106, 107, 108, 109, 110, 111, 112, 113, 123
Connecticut, 10, 13, 33, 60
Constitutional Convention, 57, 82, 85
Constitution, U.S., 57, 58, 67, 71, 72, 74, 77, 78, 79, 80, 81, 82, 88, 90, 91, 102, 104, 105, 107, 108, 118, 132
Continental Army, viii, 25, 26, 28, 31, 43, 44, 123
Cornwallis, Charles, 29
COVID-19, 114

INDEX

Dartmouth, 12
Deacon Hubbard, 44
Declaration Committee, 33
Declaration of Independence, 32, 33, 40, 42, 136
Declaratory Act, 9
Delaware, 60
Delaware River, 31, 48
District of Columbia, 67, 109
Douglass, Robert, 19
Duche', Jacob, 24
East India Company, 11, 12
Edwards, Jonathan, 4
Eleanor, 12
Elizabeth I (queen), 1
England, 11, 12, 15, 29, 45, 46, 53
Europe, 31, 45, 118, 123
First Continental Congress, 16, 24
France, 46, 117
Franklin, Benjamin, 5, 10, 33, 57, 79, 80, 82, 114
French and Indian War, 7
French West Indies, 6
Galloway, Charles, 3
General Assembly of Connecticut, 30
George III (king), 8, 51
Georgia, 60
Gerry, Elbridge, 117
Gettysburg Address, 138
Great Awakening, 4
Great Britain, 4, 5, 32, 35, 39, 41, 45
Greenwood, John, 1
Hamilton, Alexander, 83, 127
Harvard, 115

INDEX

Henry, Patrick, 8, 16, 23
Henry VIII (king), 2
Holland, 1
Home, Henry, 5
Honeyman, John, 48
House of Burgesses, 8
House of Representatives, U.S., 59, 60, 64, 65, 70, 99, 107, 110, 111
Howe, Richard, 42
Howe, William, 29, 52
Hutchinson, Thomas, 12
Israel, 130, 134
Jackson, Andrew, 137
Jefferson, Thomas, 23, 33, 40, 47, 85, 89, 115, 116, 117, 118, 119, 122, 123, 124, 125, 126, 134, 135
Jersey, HMS, 56
Katherine of Aragon, 2
Knox, Henry, 54
Lafayette, Gilbert du Motier, Marquis de, 83
Lee, Francis Lightfoot, 23
Lee, Richard Henry, 23, 32, 33
Lexington, Massachusetts, 18, 19, 21
Lexinton, Battle of, 19
Lexington Common, 17
Lieutenant Sutherland, 21
Lincoln, Abraham, 137, 138
Livingston, Robert, 33
Long Island, New York, 25
Madison, James, 113, 115, 118, 137
Marblehead, Massachusetts, 15
Marlborough, Massachusetts, 130
Maryland, 40, 60, 136

INDEX

Mason, George, 85
Massachusetts, 6, 10, 12, 15, 16, 17, 18, 33, 60
Massachusetts Government Act, 15
Massachusetts Provincial Congress, 130
Mayflower, 128
Mayhew, Jonathan, 114
Methodist, 3
Militia of Massachusettes, 132
Molasses Act, 6
Morse, Jedidiah, 133
Morse, Samuel, 133
Mr. Davis, 12
Muhlenburg, John, 44
Navy, U.S., 66, 72
Netherlands, 1
Newell, Timothy, 43
New England, 29
New Hampshire, 47, 60
New Jersey, 60
New London, Connecticut, 53
New York, 10, 26, 28, 33, 60
New York City, New York, 54
North Carolina, 60
Oliver, Andrew, 8
Paine, Thomas, 44, 48, 114
Parker, John, 18, 19, 20, 21
Parliament, 1, 7, 8, 9, 10, 11, 15, 16, 51, 53
Pennsylvania, 3, 33, 60
Penn, William, 3
Philadelphia, Pennsylvannia, 16, 24, 41
Pinckney, Charles, 83
Pitcairn, John, 21

INDEX

Pitt, William, 9, 51
Prescott, Richard, 29
President of the Constitutional Convention, 57
President of the Senate, U.S., 61, 70, 99
President *pro tempore*, U.S., 61, 110, 111
President, U.S., 61, 64, 65, 69, 70, 71, 72, 73, 74, 98, 99, 100, 101, 102, 106, 107, 108, 109, 110, 111, 112, 113, 124, 134, 137
President of Yale, 30
Prime Minister, GB, 9
Princeton, New Jersey, 31
Providence Plantations, 60
Quaker, 3, 4
Quartering Act, 16
Rall, Johann, 48, 49
Representative, U.S., 59, 60, 62, 63, 70, 79, 101, 102, 106, 109, 110, 112
Revere, Paul, 18
Rhode Island, 10, 60
Rush, Benjamin, 135
Salem, Massachusetts, 15
Scotland, 5
Second Continental Congress, 32, 33, 39, 40, 41, 47
Senate, U.S., 59, 60, 61, 64, 65, 70, 71, 73, 78, 99, 100, 104, 107, 110, 111
Senator, U.S., 60, 61, 62, 63, 70, 73, 79, 100, 102, 104, 106, 109, 110, 112
Sessions, Robert, 12
Seven Years' War, 7
Shays' Rebellion, 123
Sherman, Roger, 33
Smith, Abigail Adams, 126

INDEX

Smith, William S., 126
Sons of Liberty, 8
South Carolina, 60, 83
Spain, 46
Speaker of the House, U.S., 60, 110, 111
Stamp Act, 7, 8, 9, 115
Stamp Act Congress, 8
Stiles, Ezra, 30
Sugar Act, 7
Supreme Court, 66, 73, 74, 75
Tallmadge, Benjamin, 25, 28, 54
Taxation of the Colonies Act, 53
Tea Act, 11
The American Crisis, 48
The Holy Bible, 3, 44
Tower of London, 3
Townshend Acts, 9
Trenton, New Jersey, 48, 49
Trenton, Battle of, 49
Tyler Sr., John, 124
United States, 31, 39, 55, 57, 58, 59, 60, 61, 62, 63, 64, 65, 66, 67, 68, 69, 70, 71, 72, 73, 74, 75, 77, 78, 79, 87, 88, 98, 99, 100, 101, 102, 103, 104, 105, 107, 109, 110, 112
United States Treasury, 63, 68, 69
University of Texas, 113
Vice President, 61, 70, 71, 72, 74, 98, 99, 100, 101, 102, 106, 107, 109, 110, 111, 112
Virginia, 8, 33, 47, 60, 85
Virginia Convention, 16
Virginia Legislature, 23
War for Independence, 17
Warren, James, 131

INDEX

Washington, George, viii, 25, 26, 27, 28, 31, 48, 49, 54, 57, 83, 132
Webster, Noah, 120, 126, 137
Whitehall, New York, 55
Whitfield, George, 4
Wood, Sylvannus, 19, 21
Wood, Will, 3
Yorktown, Virginia, 53

i   *"General Orders, 2 July 1776"*, Founders Online, National Archives (at: https://founders.archives.gov/documents/Washington/03-05-02-0117) (accessed February 4, 2021)

1   David Barton, *The Jefferson Lies*, (Washington: WND Books, 2016), 157-158

2   Ibid., 157

3   Ibid.

4   Ibid., 158

5   Ibid.

6   Ibid.

7   *"William Penn Biography"*, PennsburyManor.org (at: https://www.pennsburymanor.org/history/william-penn) (accessed March 27, 2021)

8   *The American Patriot's Bible*, Richard G. Lee, editor, (Minneapolis: Thomas Nelson, Inc., 2009), I-17 and I-18

9   Ibid., I-18

10   *"From Benjamin Franklin to Lord Kames, 25 February 1767"*, Founders Online, National Archives (at: https://founders.archives.gov/documents/Franklin/01-14-02-0032) (accessed February 20, 2021)

11   *Patrick Henry voices American opposition to British policy*, History.com (at: https://www.history.com/this-day-in-history/patrick-henry-voices-american-opposition-to-british-policy) (accessed February 3, 2021)

12   Arthur D. Pierce, *Smugglers' Woods: Jaunts and Journeys in Colonial and Revolutionary New Jersey*, (New Brunswick: Rutgers University Press, 1960), 9-10

13   Ibid., 10, 14

14   *"From John Adams to William Tudor Sr., 11 August 1818"*, Founders Online, National Archives (at: https://founders.archives.gov/documents/Adams/99-

02-02-6959) (accessed March 24, 2021)
15 *Stamp Act*, History.com (at: https://www.history.com/topics/american-revolution/stamp-act) (accessed January 26, 2021)
16 Based on: Answers.com (at: https://www.answers.com/Q/How_much_was_a_penny_in_1765_worth) (accessed January 23, 2021I); Pounds To Dollars (at: https://poundstodollars.co.uk/) (accessed February, 3, 2021)
17 *Stamp Act*, History.com (at: https://www.history.com/topics/american-revolution/stamp-act) (accessed January 26, 2021)
18 Ibid.
19 Ibid.
20 Ibid.
21 Ibid.
22 Ibid.
23 Bill O'Reilly and Martin Dugard, *Killing England*, (New York: Henry Holt and Company, 2017), 173-175
24 *Townshend Acts*, History.com (at: https://www.history.com/topics/american-revolution/townshend-acts) (accessed January 23, 2021)
25 Ibid.
26 Ibid.
27 Ibid.
28 *Boston Massacre*, History.com (at: https://www.history.com/topics/american-revolution/boston-massacre) (accessed January 22, 2021)
29 Ibid.
30 *"From John Adams to James Burgh, 28 December 1774"*, Founders Online, National Archives (at: https://founders.archives.gov/documents/Adams/06-

02-02-0066) (accessed March 24, 2021)
31 *Townshend Acts*, History.com (at: https://www.history.com/topics/american-revolution/townshend-acts) (accessed January 23, 2021)
32 *Tea Act*, History.com (at: https://www.history.com/topics/american-revolution/tea-act) (accessed January 23, 2021)
33 Ibid.
34 Ibid.
35 *Boston Tea Party*, History.com (at: https://www.history.com/topics/american-revolution/boston-tea-party) (accessed February 3. 2021)
36 Ibid.
37 *The American Revolutionaries: A History In Their Own Words 1750-1800*, Milton Meltzer, editor, (New York: HarperCollins Publishers, 1987), 50-51
38 *"1773. Decr. 17th.,"*, Founders Online, National Archives (at: https://founders.archives.gov/documents/Adams/01-02-02-0003-0008-0001) (accessed March 17, 2021)
39 Kennedy Hickman, *"American Revolution: The Intolerable Acts"*, ThoughtCo, October 2, 2020 (at: https://www.thoughtco.com/the-intolerable-acts-2361386) (accessed January 23, 2021)
40 Ibid.
41 Ibid.
42 Ibid.
43 Ibid.
44 Ibid.
45 Ibid.
46 *The American Patriot's Bible*, Richard G. Lee, editor, (Minneapolis: Thomas Nelson, Inc., 2009), 951, 1345
47 *"Revere and Dawes warn of British attack"*,

History.com (at: https://www.history.com/this-day-in-history/revere-and-dawes-warn-of-british-attack) (accessed March 18, 2021)

48 Arthur Bernon Tourtellot, *Lexington and Concord: The Beginning of the War of the American Revolution*, (New York: W. W. Norton & Company, 1959), 123

49 *Battles of Lexington and Concord*, History.com (at: https://www.history.com/topics/american-revolution/battles-of-lexington-and-concord) (accessed March 18, 2021)

50 *The American Revolutionaries: A History In Their Own Words 1750-1800*, Milton Meltzer, editor, (New York: HarperCollins Publishers, 1987), 53-54

51 Arthur Bernon Tourtellot, *Lexington and Concord: The Beginning of the War of the American Revolution*, (New York: W. W. Norton & Company, 1959), 131

52 Thomas Jefferson, *The Works of Thomas Jefferson*, Paul Leicester Ford, editor, (New York and London: G.P. Putnam's Sons, 1904), Vol. II, "Notice of Fast", June 1774 (at: https://oll.libertyfund.org/title/jefferson-the-works-vol-2-1771-1779#lf0054-02_head_018) (accessed February 4, 2021)

53 David Barton, *The Jefferson Lies*, (Washington: WND Books, 2016), 168

54 *The American Patriot's Bible*, Richard G. Lee, editor, (Minneapolis: Thomas Nelson, Inc., 2009), 673

55 Mary Stockwell, Ph.D., *"Battle of Long Island"*, George Washington's Mount Vernon (at: https://www.mountvernon.org/library/digitalhistory/digital-encyclopedia/article/battle-of-long-island/) (accessed January 24, 2021)

56 *The American Revolutionaries: A History In Their*

Own Words 1750-1800, Milton Meltzer, editor, (New York: HarperCollins Publishers, 1987), 97-100

57 *The Deadliest Atlantic Tropical Cyclones, 1492-1996*, National Hurricane Center and Central Pacific Hurricane Center (at: https://www.nhc.noaa.gov/pastdeadlyapp1.shtml) (accessed February 2, 2021)

58 *NEMO remembers the great hurricane of 1780*, CDERA News Centre (at: https://web.archive.org/web/20131004223823/http://www.cdera.org/cunews/news/saint_lucia/article_1314.php) (accessed February 2, 2021)

59 Ibid.

60 Wayne Neely, *"The Great Hurricane of 1780: The Story of the Greatest and Deadliest Hurricane of the Caribbean and the Americas"*, (United Kingdon: iUniverse, 2012), 126 (at: https://www.google.com/books/edition/_/NUrOfm9zt0gC?hl=en&gbpv=1&pg=PA126) (accessed February 2, 2021)

61 AmericanRevolution.org, *Chester*, 1778 (at: https://www.americanrevolution.org/war_songs/warsongs61.php) (accessed February 4, 2021)

62 The Charter of Brown University (Providence: Akerman-Standard Press, 1945), 6 (at: https://web.archive.org/web/20120202082531/http://www.brown.edu/Administration/Corporation/downloads/charter-of-brown-university.pdf) (accessed February 4, 2021); Lewis Sheldon Welch and Walter Camp, *Yale, Her Campus, Class-rooms, and* Athletics (United States: L.C. Page, Inc, 1899), 398 (at: https://www.google.com/books/edition/Yale_Her_Campus_Class_rooms_and_Athletic/V8wWAAAAIAAJ?hl=en&gbpv=1&bsq=Ezra%20Stiles) (accessed February 4, 2021)

63 *The American Patriot's Bible*, Richard G. Lee, editor, (Minneapolis: Thomas Nelson, Inc., 2009), 1130

64 *"Resolution of Independence Moved by R. H. Lee for the Virginia Delegation, 7 June 1776"*, Founders Online, National Archives (at: https://founders.archives.gov/documents/Jefferson/01-01-02-0159) (accessed February 15, 2021)

65 *Congress appoints Committee of Five to draft the Declaration of Independence*, History.com (at: https://www.history.com/this-day-in-history/congress-appoints-committee-of-five-to-draft-the-declaration-of-independence) (accessed March 8, 2021)

66 *"From John Adams to Timothy Pickering, 6 August 1822"*, Fouders Online, National Archives (at: https://founders.archives.gov/documents/Adams/99-02-02-7674) (accessed March 8, 2021)

67 *Thomas Jefferson and the Declaration of Independence*, Monticello.org (at: https://www.monticello.org/thomas-jefferson/jefferson-s-three-greatest-achievements/the-declaration/jefferson-and-the-declaration) (accessed March 8, 2021)

68 *"From Thomas Jefferson to Henry Lee, 8 May 1825"*, Founders Online, National Archives (at: https://founders.archives.gov/documents/Jefferson/98-01-02-5212) (accessed March 24, 2021)

69 *"From John Adams to Samuel Chase, 1 July 1776"*, Ibid. (at: https://founders.archives.gov/documents/Adams/06-04-02-0142) (accessed February 15, 2021)

70 *"John Adams to Abigail Adams, 3 July 1776"*, Ibid. (at: https://founders.archives.gov/documents/Adams/04-02-02-0016) (accessed February 14, 2021)

71 Bill O'Reilly and Martin Dugard, *Killing England*, (New York: Henry Holt and Company, 2017), 111
72 *The American Patriot's Bible*, Richard G. Lee, editor, (Minneapolis: Thomas Nelson, Inc., 2009), I-15
73 Ibid.
74 *The American Revolutionaries: A History In Their Own Words 1750-1800*, Milton Meltzer, editor, (New York: HarperCollins Publishers, 1987), 67
75 *The American Patriot's Bible*, Richard G. Lee, editor, (Minneapolis: Thomas Nelson, Inc., 2009), I-16
76 Thomas Paine, *Common Sense*, (Philadelphia: Robert Bell, 1776 (at: https://www.law.gmu.edu/assets/files/academics/founders/Paine_CommonSense.pdf) (accessed March 25, 2021)
77 David Barton, *The Jefferson Lies*, (Washington: WND Books, 2016), 170-171
78 *The American Revolutionaries: A History In Their Own Words 1750-1800*, Milton Meltzer, editor, (New York: HarperCollins Publishers, 1987), 76-77
79 Thomas Paine, *The American Crisis*, Pennsylvania Journal, December 19, 1776 (at: https://thefederalistpapers.org/wp-content/uploads/2013/08/The-American-Crisis-by-Thomas-Paine-.pdf) (accessed February 4, 2021)
80 *The American Revolutionaries: A History In Their Own Words 1750-1800*, Milton Meltzer, editor, (New York: HarperCollins Publishers, 1987), 101
81 Kennedy Hickman, *"American Revolution: Battle of Trenton"*, ThoughtCo, August 26, 2020 (at: https://www.thoughtco.com/battle-of-trenton-2360634) (accessed March 22, 2021)
82 *The American Revolutionaries: A History In Their Own Words 1750-1800*, Milton Meltzer, editor,

(New York: HarperCollins Publishers, 1987), 109-110

83 Bill O'Reilly and Martin Dugard, *Killing England*, (New York: Henry Holt and Company, 2017), 173
84 Ibid, 174-175
85 *The Taxation Of Colonies Act~1778*, Historical Documents of the United States of America (at: https://www.motherbedford.com/HistoricalDocuments63.htm) (accessed January 23, 2021)
86 Bill O'Reilly and Martin Dugard, *Killing England*, (New York: Henry Holt and Company, 2017),
87 *The American Revolutionaries: A History In Their Own Words 1750-1800*, Milton Meltzer, editor, (New York: HarperCollins Publishers, 1987), 182-184
88 *American Revolution Facts*, American Battlefield Trust (at: https://www.battlefields.org/learn/articles/american-revolution-faqs) (accessed February 13, 2021)
89 *The American Patriot's Bible*, Richard G. Lee, editor, (Minneapolis: Thomas Nelson, Inc., 2009), 727
90 *The American Revolutionaries: A History In Their Own Words 1750-1800*, Milton Meltzer, editor, (New York: HarperCollins Publishers, 1987), 193-196
91 *The American Patriot's Bible*, Richard G. Lee, editor, (Minneapolis: Thomas Nelson, Inc., 2009), 1251
92 Ibid.
93 Ibid.
94 *"From George Washington to Lafayette, 7 February 1788"*, Founders Online, National Archives (at: https://founders.archives.gov/documents/Washington/04-06-02-0079) (accessed March 25, 2021)
95 *The American Patriot's Bible*, Richard G. Lee,

editor, (Minneapolis: Thomas Nelson, Inc., 2009), 17

96 Ibid.

97 *"III. First Inaugural Address, 4 March 1801"*, Founders Online, National Archives (at: https://founders.archives.gov/documents/Jefferson/01-33-02-0116-0004) (accessed February 4, 2021)

98 Evan Andrews, *"The Strange Saga of the 27th Amendment"*, History.com, August 31, 2018 (at: https://www.history.com/news/the-strange-case-of-the-27th-amendment) (accessed January 31, 2021)

99 Ibid.

100 Ibid.

101 Ibid.

102 Rush Limbaugh, *See, I Told You So*, (New York: Pocket Books, 1993), xvii

103 *"Franklin's Contributions to the Conference on February 17: Four Drafts, 1775"*, Founders Online, National Archives (at: https://founders.archives.gov/documents/Franklin/01-21-02-0269) (accessed February 4, 2021)

104 *The American Patriot's Bible*, Richard G. Lee, editor, (Minneapolis: Thomas Nelson, Inc., 2009), 354

105 Thomas Jefferson, *The Political Writings of Thomas Jefferson*, Merrill D. Peterson, editor, (Chapel Hill: The University of North Carolina Press, 1993), 162, to John B. Colvin on September 20, 1810

106 Ibid., 79-80, to James Madison on January 30, 1787

107 The Editors of Encyclopaedia, *"John Cartwright"*, Britannica, September 19, 2020 (at: https://www.britannica.com/biography/John-Cartwright) (accessed May 1, 2021)

108 Thomas Jefferson, *The Political Writings of Thomas Jefferson*, Merrill D. Peterson, editor,

(Chapel Hill: The University of North Carolina Press, 1993), 210, to Major John Cartwright on June 5, 1824

109 Ibid., 133, to Elbridge Gerry on January 26, 1799

110 Ibid., 84, to James Madison on December 20, 1787

111 *"From Thomas Jefferson to Peter Carr, 19 August 1785"*, Founders Online, National Archives (at: https://founders.archives.gov/documents/Jefferson/01-08-02-0319) (accessed March 25, 2021)

112 *The American Patriot's Bible*, Richard G. Lee, editor, (Minneapolis: Thomas Nelson, Inc., 2009), 290

113 Ibid., 91

114 Ibid., 353

115 Thomas Jefferson, *The Political Writings of Thomas Jefferson*, Merrill D. Peterson, editor, (Chapel Hill: The University of North Carolina Press, 1993), 44, A Bill for the More General Diffusion of Knowledge (1778)

116 Ibid., 78, to Edward Carrington on January 16, 1787

117 Ibid., 152-153, to John Tyler on June 28, 1804

118 Ibid., 180, to Colonel Charles Yancey on January 6, 1816

119 Ibid., 81, to William S. Smith on November 13, 1787

120 Patriotism, Merriam-Webster.com (at: https://www.merriam-webster.com/dictionary/patriotism?src=search-dict-box) (accessed January 15, 2021)

121 *The American Patriot's Bible*, Richard G. Lee, editor, (Minneapolis: Thomas Nelson, Inc., 2009), 406

122 *"The Farmer Refuted, &c., [23 February] 1775"*, Founders Online, National Archives (at: https://founders.archives.gov/documents/Hamilton/0

1-01-02-0057) (accessed May 4, 2021)
123 *The American Patriot's Bible*, Richard G. Lee, editor, (Minneapolis: Thomas Nelson, Inc., 2009), 411
124 *"John Adams to Abigail Adams, 26 April 1777"*, Founders Online, National Archives (at: https://founders.archives.gov/documents/Adams/04-02-02-0169) (accessed February 5, 2021)
125 *The American Patriot's Bible*, Richard G. Lee, editor, (Minneapolis: Thomas Nelson, Inc., 2009), 836
126 Ibid., 1267
127 *"John Adams to Zabdiel Adams, 21 June 1776"*, Founders Online, National Archives (at: https://founders.archives.gov/documents/Adams/04-02-02-0011) (accessed February 4, 2021)
128 *The American Patriot's Bible*, Richard G. Lee, editor, (Minneapolis: Thomas Nelson, Inc., 2009), 276
129 *"Farewell Address, 19 September 1796"*, Founders Online, National Archives (at: https://founders.archives.gov/documents/Washington/99-01-02-00963) (accessed February 4, 2021)
130 *"From John Adams to Massachusetts Militia, 11 October 1798"*, Ibid (at: https://founders.archives.gov/documents/Adams/99-02-02-3102) (accessed February 4, 2021)
131 *The American Patriot's Bible*, Richard G. Lee, editor, (Minneapolis: Thomas Nelson, Inc., 2009), 659
132 The Editors of Encyclopaedia, *"Jedidiah Morse"*, Britannica, August 19, 2020 (at: https://www.britannica.com/biography/Jedidiah-Morse) (accessed May 3, 2021)
133 David Barton, *The Jefferson Lies*, (Washington: WND Books, 2016), 174

134 *"Second Inaugural Address, 4 March 1805"*, Founders Online, National Archives (at: https://founders.archives.gov/documents/Jefferson/99-01-02-1302) (acceseed March 25, 2021)

135 *"John Adams to Thomas Jefferson, 28 June 1813"*, Ibid. (at: https://founders.archives.gov/documents/Jefferson/03-06-02-0208) (accessed March 25, 2021)

136 *"To Thomas Jefferson from Benjamin Rush, 22 August 1800"*, Ibid. (at: https://founders.archives.gov/documents/Jefferson/01-32-02-0072) (accessed March 25, 2021)

137 *The American Patriot's Bible*, Richard G. Lee, editor, (Minneapolis: Thomas Nelson, Inc., 2009), I-12

138 Ibid., 134

139 Rush Limbaugh, *See, I Told You So*, (New York: Pocket Books, 1993), 73

140 Andrew Jackson, *Farewell Address*, March 4, 1837, Library of Congress (at: https://www.loc.gov/resource/maj.04135_0001_0048/?st=gallery) (accessed March 25, 2021)

www.ingramcontent.com/pod-product-compliance
Lightning Source LLC
Chambersburg PA
CBHW051436290426
44109CB00016B/1574